Dusty Trails

Glorianne Weigand

Cover photo: Taken in 1907 of Benjamin Franklin Studley with his horse "Teddy Roosevelt" and carriage in front of the barn built in 1885 which is still in use on the 101 Ranch today.

ISBN 0-9644141-0-4

Printed by
Maverick Publications, Inc.
P.O. Box 5007
Bend, Oregon 97708

Acknowledgements

In appreciation of those I interviewed and who were willing to share their stories, experiences, pictures and memories of themselves or their families. Thank you to everyone that has been so helpful in this venture.

The Studley story:	Norma Studley Weigand, John Poytress and Stan Weigand
The Babcock story:	Ruth Babcock Bouse, Dora Babcock Carpenter, Opal Babcock Conners and Dorotha Babcock
The Joiner story:	Albert and Lillian Joiner
The Stevenson story:	Joe and Ruby Stevenson
The McGarva story:	Duane and Dixie McGarva, Kenneth and Jackie McGarva
The Kramer story:	Dorotha Gerig Kramer, Orma Kramer Albaugh, Buster Bouse, Bunny Carmichael
The Crum story:	Orville, Hiram, Allan and Donald Crum, Irene Crum, Norman and Betty Taylor and Barbara Crum Joiner
The Bennett story:	Hilda and Alva Bennett, Janice and Dale Flux
The Shaw story:	Monroe, Bob and Billie Shaw
The Dixon story:	Clevon and Anola Dixon
The Kresge story:	Edna Kresge
The Bognuda story:	Clover Bognuda Corder, George and Kathy Corder and notes written by Lil Bognuda Lambert

The Poytress story:	John and Marjorie Poytress
The McCoy and Stone story:	Bertha McCoy
The Thompson story:	Bill and Louella Thompson
The Shepherd story:	Charlie Shepherd
The Wilcox story:	Verna Wilcox, Corky Wilcox Saltzman, Betty Wilcox Taylor and Richard Taylor
The Swain story:	Roy Swain

Some of those that were interviewed have already left us and we are thankful we were able to capture their stories and memories in this book while they were still with us.

Some of the stories have been edited from their original manuscript as they were printed in *The Nevada Rancher*.

Dedication

I dedicate this book to my husband Stan, who encourages me to write the memories of these great people who are willing to share them with us.

To our sons Doug and Scott, Thanks.

I also dedicate this book to Glenn Nader who had the faith in me that I could write the stories the way they were told to me. He started it all.

Table of Contents

1. The 101 Ranch   1
   Studley and Weigand

2. Brave Pioneers of the Big Valley   9
   The Ernie Babcock Family

3. A Love for Farming   17
   Albert and Lillian Joiner

4. A Cattleman and a Horse Lover   24
   Joe and Ruby Stevenson

5. The McGarva Clan: Stewards of the Land   31
   Duane and Kenneth McGarva

6. Louis Kramer Began Ranching Legacy In Big Valley   38
   The Kramer Ranch

7. The Crum Meat Company 1932-1971   47
   The Merton Crum Family

8. A True Cowboy and His Pioneer Lady   56
   Alva & Hilda Bennett and Janice & Dale Flux

9. Somewhere Between Nevada and the Ocean   62
   Monroe Shaw

10. Tales of an MC Cow Boss   72
    Clevon and Anola Dixon

11. Pioneers In an Untamed Land   83
    The Kresge Family

12. **The Bognuda Bunch From Little Valley**   91
    Ned, Josie, Clover and Lil Bognuda

13. **Cowboy Reflections**   101
    John Poytress

14. **The Stones And McCoy Pioneers**   106
    Earl McCoy and Henry Norton Stone

15. **The Thompson Ranch**   115
    Bill Thompson

16. **Free as a Breeze, and Wild as a Sagebrush**   120
    Charlie Shepherd

17. **Wilcox Ranch Survives Mt. Lassen Eruption**   126
    Verna Wilcox

18. **There Was Never a Bronco Too Tough**   137
    Roy Swain

The 101 Ranch

A gentle rain was falling that early spring day in April, 1869 when Benjamin Franklin Studley first brought his young wife, Celia Jane and their two year old daughter Hattie Ann to Big Valley and the ranch they would homestead. In the wagon behind them, drawn by a strong team of horses like their own, was Ben's brother, Silas and his family. This was the beginning of the 101 Ranch five generations and 125 years ago.

Benjamin Franklin Studley was born in 1837 in Woldoboro, Maine. In 1855, when he was 18 years old, he headed to the gold fields of California. He and his brother came by boat around Cape Horn into San Francisco. The trip was rough and the ship was listing dangerously, so they had to throw their possessions overboard. He had only what he carried in his hands. They started their life in the wild west in Sacramento, then moved to Yreka, California. This is where he met his wife, Celia Jane Stanley and they were married in Hawkinsville, California on October 19, 1865. There, he was a carpenter, miner, butcher and owned a saloon.

Ben heard the news that Big Valley to the east of Mount Shasta had been surveyed and was open for homesteaders. Ben and Silas came to set up their claim. They built a small cabin, then went back for their families.

Celia Jane was afraid of the Indians as they were seen lurking nearby. She was afraid they would kidnap their child. The Indians would soon leave when they saw the white men working in the fields.

Ben homesteaded the north 160 acres and Silas homesteaded the south 160 acres. This began the present 101 Ranch that is situated three miles southwest of the town of Adin. The 101 brand was claimed at once and has been in constant use for 125 years in the same family. Sheep at that time were branded on the nose and a small "s" was used for that purpose.

At that time there was only one other cabin on the west side of the valley. They built another log home and at once started to re-route the Willow Creek that ran the full length of the lush meadows to irrigate more of the highland. At that time the only way to dig a ditch was by hand. Some of the local Indians were hired to do this job. The Indians called the ditch "Skookum Chuck",

1

Wedding picture of Benjamin Franklin Studley and Celia Jane Stanley married at Hawkinsville, California, October 19, 1865.

which in Indian language meant "good food". The local Indian camp was not far from the ranch and many Indians would ride their horses or walk to the Studley homestead to be served a bountiful breakfast of biscuits, meat and mush and lots of strong coffee. Ben would choose several to work that day and the rest would return to camp. The next morning they again would all return for breakfast and again the workers would be chosen and the rest went home with a happy heart and full stomach.

On October 15, 1869, Celia Jane gave birth to their first son Frank. Not only was he their first son, he was the first white boy born in Big Valley. There had only been Indian babies born up to that time. Frank was born in the log cabin that is still standing today and has been restored and preserved and turned into a museum. After Frank, two more children were born, Eva and Clarence.

On March 4, 1870, water rights were claimed on the ranch from Willow Creek. On March 15, 1873, Ulysses S. Grant, president of the United States, signed the original patent to the 101 Ranch to homesteader Benjamin Franklin Studley. Silas J. Studley's original patent was also signed by President Grant on August 20, 1875.

In 1882 a larger home was built on the ranch. Soon after, in 1883, Celia Jane gave birth to the couple's fifth child and complications set in and the mother and child both died. Celia Jane was buried in the Adin cemetery with her baby in her arms.

This pioneer lady had raised her family for fourteen years in a small one room cabin. She died only a few months after moving to her new home she had waited so long for.

In 1876, Silas sold out to Ben and moved his family to Goose Lake near Lakeview, Oregon. This made the 101 Ranch, now owned by Ben Studley, a total of 320 acres of prime farm land and lush meadow.

The following are the contents of a letter written to a cousin, Mr. Alden Wiley, S.Q. Waldoboro, Maine, October, 1888 from Ben.

> Dear friend Alden, you must excuse me for not answering your letter sooner. My wife died about five years ago, I have four children. One girl, Hattie, 22 years old, one boy, Frank, 19 years old, one girl, Eva, 15 years old and one boy, Clarence, 11 years old. I am farming here and raising stock. I have 100 head of cattle, 20 head of horses and 800 head of sheep. I cut 500 to 600 tons of hay each year. I have 560 acres in one body. I bought 160 acres this summer. I shall hay 80 acres more this fall. We have to feed here two to four months in the winter and we have a few pretty cold days. Silas lives about one hundred miles from here. There is quartz mining about fifteen miles from here. I am doing first rate. I would like to go back and see the folks if it were not for leaving my children. I would like to bring the folks out here. I have a good house and two barns. My oldest girl is married. My youngest

girl keeps house for me and the boys. Tell mother I am ashamed for not writing to her but I haven't written to anyone there for over twenty years. Write to me and tell me who is dead and who is living, that I asked. Direct to Adin, Modoc County, California. B.F. Studley.

On December 24, 1893, Frank Studley married a neighbor girl, Hattie Kelly. To that union two girls were born, Marie and Norma.

On September 27, 1893, Ben married for the second time. His new bride was the niece of his deceased wife. She was a widow with two children. His new wife was not use to the hard life of the ranch and was not happy there. She persuaded Ben to give up the ranch and move to Reno, Nevada. At that time he was seventy two years old and his health was failing. His younger wife, Eva, wanted to enjoy the city life and put her daughter into nursing training there. Ben died two years later in 1912 at the age of 74. Some say he died from a broken heart of having to give up the life and ranch he loved. He was buried in Reno, not returned to Big Valley as he had wished.

A Mr. L. Grater had leased the ranch in 1911 and kept on taking care of it until 1914. The 101 Ranch then fell into a series of renters for the next five years. Ben's four children and Eva's two children could never come to an agreement as to who should rent the ranch or what should happen to it. A Mr. Emerson was appointed as the administrator by Mrs. Studley. He was noted in a letter from a Susanville attorney as being an unfit and unproper person, but nothing could be done about his appointment.

A son of Eva Studley, Jesse Campbell, was an attorney in Reno and also made life miserable for the Studley heirs as did Mr. Emerson. In the five years renters used the land and buildings, they never repaired or replaced any fences or buildings and soon the ranch was getting very run down.

In letters written to Frank Studley in 1914, 1915 and 1916 from Jesse Campbell, he kept urging for a long term lease to one rancher from the Sierra Valley. He even threatened to sue Frank if he did not lease the ranch to this man.

Neither Frank's sisters or his brother, who was teaching at Chico State College, wanted anything to do with the ranch. Frank had a dry land ranch south of Adin himself, so he really did not have the time or energy to run the 101 Ranch. Finally after several unsuccessful renters and the persistence of his step-brother, Frank bought out the other heirs and sold his ranch. Jesse wanted to buy the 101 Ranch himself, but Frank's sisters would have nothing to do with him owning their father's ranch.

In 1914, Frank had put up the hay on his father's estate. In 1915, Cannon and Hastings put up the hay and in the winter, Mr. and Mrs. Cannon moved into the Studley home and fed their cattle the hay. From 1916 to 1918, K.C. Campbell put up the hay and sold it to Henry Caldwell of Canby. Mr. Caldwell

Stan Weigand 4th generation on the 101 Ranch.

drove his cattle from Canby those winters and stayed there and fed their cattle the purchased hay.

In March 1919, Frank and Hattie Studley moved to the 101 Ranch with their two daughters, Marie who was 21 years old and Norma who was 15 years old. Frank was fifty years old at this time and this large ranch was almost too much for him. He had malaria when he was younger and he was not as strong as some men his age. His wife Hattie said that the ranch came to him too late in life.

Frank purchased the original homestead and added some acreage from the heirs and he then added more purchased land and the ranch totaled 2200 acres. Quite a few acres were added by paying back taxes or buying Indian land. Then he bought a piece of land from Dewey Dibble, a local Indian. Dewey wrote a letter in 1943 that said: Mr. Studley, will you please send me ten dollars, I got to buy flour for me. Dewey Dibble.

Food preserving was a long and laborious task. In early years, a man came through the valley taking orders for fruit trees. Ben ordered many apple, pear and plum trees and planted a good sized orchard. Huge crocks of apple butter and pear and plum preserves lined the tables of the cool store room.

5

Apple cider was made by the barrel full. A large garden yielded potatoes, carrots and cabbage for the winter use. Hogs would be butchered six at a time and the hams, bacons and shoulders were cured in barrels of brine and smoked. Beef was butchered and hung at night and put in canvases in the hay during the day to keep it cool. The chickens provided the eggs and meat. The milk cow provided milk, cream, butter and cheese. There was enough cream to make butter and haul it to the Hayden Hill miners. It was left at the foot of Hayden Hill in a cold box built over a spring until someone came by and hauled it up the hill. At times the Studleys milked up to thirty cows.

In 1927, Frank and Hattie moved to the town of Adin when they leased the ranch to Glyne Johnson and Darrel Traugh. When Glyne married Lois Harbert, Darrel left to go his own way. The Johnsons stayed on for several years then moved on. Glyne, later in life, was the Modoc County sheriff. In 1934 and 1935, Frank and Hattie moved back to run the ranch and Thomas Wolter worked for them as he had worked for Glyne. In 1936, when Tom married, he leased the ranch. The Studley family moved back to town. In 1942 Mr. Studley wrote to John Poytress who had worked the summers on the neighboring Weigand Ranch and asked him if he would like to lease the

Branding time on the 101 Ranch.
Doug and Scott Weigand, 5th generation on 101 Ranch. 1978.

6

Stan and Glorianne Weigand.

ranch. John and Marjorie Poytress moved back to Adin and ran the 101 Ranch for fourteen years.

In 1941, Frank and Hattie had a home built on the ranch right next to the neighboring ranch where their daughter Norma and her husband Lawrence Weigand lived. Hattie passed away in 1949 at the age of 79 and Frank passed away in 1952 at the age of 83. At that time, their daughters, Marie Wright of Oakland, and Norma Weigand inherited the ranch. This made the third generation that owned the ranch. The Poytress family left in 1955. Norma's daughter Avis and her husband Lee Crews ran the ranch until 1960. At that time Norma's husband Lawrence and son Stan leased the ranch for three years. After that, Stan and his wife Glorianne purchased the ranch and moved there with their two small sons, Doug and Scott in 1963. This made the fourth and fifth generation to live on the 101 Ranch.

In the early years, many men were hired to cut, rake and stack the huge loose hay stacks and drive the teams of horses. A cook was always hired to help with the meals. Now the hay is put up by two or three people and there is no extra cook. We do it ourselves and spend many hours horse back as we ride the range to tend to our cattle. In early years, the cattle were left to roam the vast acres of knee deep grass.

Norma, Marie, Hattie and Frank Studley in 1925.

The original log home was preserved and made into a museum on the ranch. The large home that was built in 1882 burned in 1958 taking with it many trunks of antique treasures. The house that was built in 1941 was moved to the place where the one burned down. The original barn built in 1885 still stands proudly and is used daily. Its hand hewn beams, square nails and hand carved wooden pegs are a reminder of the crude tools and methods our forefathers had to work with.

This working cattle ranch with the same 101 brand used for 125 years and five generations is a tribute to one brave man who started it all when he left his home and family in the east to pursue his dreams in the wild west.

Glorianne Weigand
April, 1993

The Babcock Family:
Brave Pioneers of the Big Valley

The nights were turning mighty cold that October in 1872 when the Babcock family ventured to Big Valley. The earthquake in Marin County in 1868 was the reason these pioneers headed north to the California Mountain Valley. The family had to camp out until they were able to cut timber and make shakes for a home. By the first of November they had built a house and small barn and hauled their wood for the winter. The weather was mild and Chester Babcock was able to till the soil and plant twenty acres of wheat.

Chester's wife Amelia had died when she was quite young and left him to raise the children, Will, Chet, Andy and Ella.

Big Valley was wide open, you could go all the way from hillside stage station at the foot of Big Valley Mountain to Adin straight across the prairie without running into a fence until you got to Willow Creek where Ben Studley had a strip of meadow under fence. Even the Cox and Clarke swamp was not fenced at that time.

Adin was the only town in the valley. Blask had a drug store, Jim Beacker had a general merchandise store, Jim Bedford had a store also. Lapoint had an old grist mill where the farmers got their grist ground.

In april 1932 Andrew Babcock wrote an account of the last sixty years, in which he describes the life and hardships of the pioneers. In the summer of 1873 they swam their teams across the river to haul the rails to fence in the twenty acres of wheat so the cattle and horses that were grazing on the prairie would not destroy it. At that time the rye grass and feed was as high as a horse's back and bunch grass was two to three feet high. Before the farmers got a chance to harvest the grain or hay crops on the river, the Kansas grasshoppers swooped down from the north and cleaned up grain, grass and gardens. They took everything in their path. They came in swarms so thick that a team would not face them against the north wind that was blowing at that time. With no hay for the Babcock cattle to eat that winter, they had to put up hay from the swamp on shares so they would have feed for their stock for the coming months.

The Babcock family started milking some dairy cows and making butter and hauling it to the bluffs, (Red Bluff). There they would trade the butter for shoes, clothes and food. After the grasshoppers, there was no grain to make flour so Chester Babcock, W. Calsion, C. Perkiss and Woolsey all rigged up a four horse team each and went to Ashland, Oregon to the Morton Milling Company for flour which they could get for thirteen dollars a thousand pounds. It took all the money the neighborhood could raise to buy three thousand pounds of flour for each team to haul. The trip took eighteen days and upon their return the flour was divided among the neighbors who helped raise the money.

There were many Indians in Big Valley at the time and you could often see five hundred or more riding across the plains horseback with eagle feathers in their hats and war paint on their faces. The Klamath Indians would come to gamble with the Pit River Indians. They would gamble off their blankets, trinkets, horses and wives.

The Modoc Indian war was in progress and more settlers were drifting into Big Valley during the summer of 1873. The families decided to put up a school house and the year seemed as normal as any other. Winter started with some rain and by New Years there was six inches of snow, and turning very cold. The river was low and it froze clear to the bottom. The snow seemed endless and the wind was unbearable. By the 15th of March nearly everyone was out of hay and the snow was two feet deep on the level and drifted six to eight feet. The Babcocks and their neighbors joined together and drove their cattle up near Willow Creek on the south slopes near the Preston Mine where they could browse on mahogany brush. They were five days getting the cattle there through the deep snow. Andrew Babcock and Dave Watson were both snow blind and froze their feet so bad they could not get their boots on. The snow laid on the ground until April. About eighty percent of the cattle perished and all the sheep died, as they were helpless in the snow. It began to look like the men were going to perish along with their stock. The people emptied their hay mattresses to save a milk cow. The cattle were too poor to eat and flour and bacon was gone. It was May tenth before there was any grass for the cows to graze.

After the hard winter and all of the snow the valley was flooded. Spring came and left most of the farmers destitute. They put in grain and gardens and headed back to Ashland to the Morton Milling Company for flour. Many settlers moved out, cursing the Big Valley.

Mild winters meant no crops the next summer and hard winters brought good crops and lots of grass if the livestock could survive the blizzards.

In 1877 Nathan Bieber put a store in and started the town of Bieber. Bill Arnett built a saloon, and Lambert put up a blacksmith shop. Mr. Ford built a hotel and a printing office. Other businesses were started and the town of Bieber was booming.

Chester's son Andrew established a blacksmith shop in Bieber and built a two story house behind the shop. In 1882 he married Amy Way, her family had crossed the plains in a covered wagon. Andrew was a blacksmith, musician, carpenter and wagon builder, farmer and rancher. After the couple were married Andy moved the home he built to the homestead near Bieber using four wagons and teams. Andy and Amy had nine children, Alfred, Milton, Harry, Rosy, Ernest, Frank, Lester, Arad and Mervin. When Chester was too old to work his homestead he handed it down to Andrew and his brothers. He had expanded his ranch enough so he could divide the place for each of his six sons. Giving them a good start with land, cattle, horses, wagon, harness and what they needed to start a ranch. Rosy being the only girl did not get any part of the ranch.

Andrew and Amy retired and one of their sons, Ernest was given a part of the ranch known as Mud Island.

Ernie was a determined man and had his mind made up like his father from the beginning he was gong to build an empire large enough to pass on to his future sons.

On February 23, 1919 Ernie married Bessie Jane Carmichael. The daughter of Allen and Elizabeth Carmichael who were the Babcocks' best friends. Bessie was born at Hayden Hill, January 27, 1900 during the big gold rush. Her father had been in an explosion in the mine that killed his partner and crushed Allen's leg. Not able to mine any longer he began a tavern at the gold mining town, later moving it to Bieber when Hayden Hill ran out of gold.

Ernie and Bessie soon started their family of sixteen children. Russell, Opal, Andrew, Lula, Raymond, Dora, Otis, Ruth, Ona, Chester, Ruby, Fern, Arnold (died in infancy), Charles, Lilly and Gloria. Ernie delivered all of the children at home by himself except for the last one and the local doctor came out to assist.

Ernie had to start expanding his ranch holdings pretty fast to have enough to pass on to his sons like he had promised.

Ernie built a small cabin for his family at Mud Flat three miles south of Bieber near the Pit River. When the family started to expand, a new large farm house was built to accommodate the large family that Ernie and Bessie were planning.

The older children went to the Juniper School which was about two miles away and across the river sloughs. They rode horseback and had to lead their horses across some planks on the sloughs or swim them across. They had to

In the back row: Russ, Andy, Bessie, Ernie.
Second row, left to right: Opal, Lula holding Chet, Raymond, Dora, Otis.
In the front row: Ruth and Ona.

open four gates on the way, until one of the neighbors who was not too kindly decided to lock the gates and the Babcock children had to walk. When they got to school there was a barn to tie their horses in during the school hours. When the weather was miserable in the winter the children would suffer from frozen ears and frost bitten fingers and toes. When it was unbearable they would sometimes stay at the Thompson Ranch with that family.

In 1933 the Juniper School was closed and the children had to go to Bieber to school. Getting to school was always an adventure. In the winter when there was snow they used a sleigh and horses, but when it melted in the spring they had to use the spring wagon to get through the mud. Usually it was Easter before they could make it to town with a car. One morning while going to school in the spring wagon the wagon hammer came out, turning the team loose with the neck yoke and double trees. The team ran straddle the Jones kids that were riding their horses ahead of the Babcock kids. Upending the horses, kids and all in a ditch full of snow. No one was hurt, but plenty scared. The team continued on to Bieber without the wagon and Babcocks. Charlie Snell caught the team and brought them back so the kids could go on to school.

Some time after the family started driving a car to school which was known as the Babcock bus they would get stuck in their long muddy lane and have to walk the rest of the way. Some days when they reached school they were so cold they could not even turn the knob to open the door.

Ernie was in the dairy business with his brothers, Lester and Arad until 1938 when he pulled out of the company. Ernie and his sons milked up to sixty cows. Milking started at 4:30 a.m. And breakfast was at 8:30 or 9:00 when the milking chores were done. When the children went to school they would have to deliver the milk and cream to the creamery at Bieber before they went to class.

The milking was done by milking machines run by a gasoline motor. Air was piped all through the cow barn to run the milking machines. Every cow had a name and a certain stanchion to stand in. They would first wash each cow's udder with hot water and some had to be hobbled to keep them from kicking the machines off. After the cows were milked with the machines, they had to be hand stripped of the last bit of milk. This is where all the kids learned to milk.

50th anniversary of Andrew and Amy Babcock, 1930.

In the back (all grandchildren): Russell, Andy, Oral, Rolene, Marjorie, Harold (holding Norma), Evelyn.
In the front: Otis, Raymond (Ruth in front), Grandma & Grandpa Babcock, Opal (holding Ona), Bobby, Lula, and Dora.

After the milking, all of the machines had to be taken apart and washed and scalded and the cow barns cleaned out. This was the job that the girls got along with all of the house chores.

Saturday was clean and wash day and all the girls got in on the chore. Water had to be pumped from the pitcher pump in the backyard. Packed to the kitchen and heated on the old wood cook stove in a big copper boiler. Then they packed the hot water to the gasoline Maytag wringer washing machine. The clothes were hung in the back yard to dry in the good weather, but in stormy weather the clothes had to hang on the back porch and upstairs to dry. While the clothes dried the house was thoroughly cleaned and scrubbed. After the clothes were dried they were folded, ironed and the beds were made. The ironing was done with the old black flat iron heated on the wood stove. Washing was a big job for fifteen kids and their parents. The girls loved to play a joke on the boys by short sheeting their beds. Baths were taken in a galvanized tub after pumping the water and heating the water on the cook stove again.

Bread baking day you would have thought you had stepped into a very large bakery. The huge bread mixing bowl was also used as a popcorn bowl for a treat for the whole family. The smell of the warm bread filled the whole house from the dining room with its long oilcloth covered dining table to the farthest bedroom in the upstairs.

A real surprise was when Ernie came home from delivering the cream and milk to the cheese factory in Bieber and he had a player piano in the milk wagon. Everyone loved to pump the pedals and listen to the beautiful music. Bessie had a beautiful voice and the children loved to hear her sing while she did her work. They would sit in the evening and Bessie would sing to them while they waited for their dad and brothers to come in from doing the milking.

The Sears and Roebuck catalog was very important to the Babcock family as that is where they ordered all of their clothes and shoes. The children hated to wear shoes in the summer time and by the time school started and the new shoes arrived they had to suffer the blisters until they got use to them.

Pranks were a part of their family life. Russ, Andy and Opal were exploring in the old woods house when they encountered a skunk. Russ picked up a board and hit the skunk in the back, and they all got sprayed. Their dad made them wade in the pond the rest of the afternoon.

Bessie was deathly afraid of snakes. The kids found a garden snake and wrapped it around the door knob, shut the screen door, knocked on the door and ran. Fern seemed to be the instigator of this prank and she could hear her mother yelling for years to come. One time when the barn was being built down near the road, Ernie told Fern and Ruby to stay at the house. Well, that was an invitation to come see what they were missing. Fern took the road, but Ruby wanted to be sneaky and not be seen so she went by the slough.

Bessie & Ernie Babcock, 1962.

This was a mistake as a porcupine had the same idea as Ruby and she and Mr. Porky had a very painful encounter.

Games and sports were played with the whole family group. The kids made their toys and trucks out of sticks, blocks and cans. Chet was the main truck and tractor builder. He could make anything. They made logging trucks and saws from can lids and would log the sunflowers down near the pig pen. One game that could have been a little dangerous was "fool around the haystack." This is where they threw pitchforks over the edge and the next guy threw it back. One time when Ruby threw it Fern didn't dodge too well and got the pitchfork in her leg.

The Big Valley school district sports department was always thrilled when a Babcock entered high school. With all their basketball and baseball games at home with their built in teams, most of them were natural athletes.

Electricity was brought into the ranch in 1945. Running water, an inside bathroom with a tub, lights and radio were all so very welcome in this large family.

Ernie gradually increased his ranch holdings to 3840 acres by buying out homesteaders and neighbors with adjoining land. In 1916 a U.S. timber claim was added, in 1920 he bought out Andrew and Amy Babcock, 1937 M.G. and W.J. Thompson, 1938 Babcock brothers, Lester Babcock and Arad Babcock, 1938 Walker Investment Company, 1939, Andrew and Adrella Babcock, 1945 Andrew Babcock estate, 1946 Rucker and Andy Kramer, 1948, Homer Jack and Carpenter, 1960, Andy Yordy and Chet Cole.

Ernie and his family worked hard on their ranch. He finally gave up the milk cows after Russ, Andy and Raymond were drafted in World War II. He then went into the beef cattle business and raised grain and hay.

It was not unusual for the boys or girls to start working in the hay field at seven years of age with a gentle old team of horses driving derrick.

In 1947 Ernie bought a new baler and a new John Deere side delivery rake. Chet started out with the new rake and a young team, Jim and Jerry. About the second day something broke on the reel of the rake, it made a loud bang and the team took off with the rake, but Chet didn't stay with them long. The rake ran over Chet, but he only had a few scratches and was knocked out. When he came to, the team and rake were half way to the house. The team made it fine, but the rake enlarged a couple of gates on the way. Ernie took over the raking job and put Chet on the back of the baler re-tieing the bales the baler had missed.

Ernie and Bessie lived and worked on the ranch until he was 70 years old and in 1962 he retired. Ernie had done as he had vowed and divided his ranch holdings among his six sons. Some brothers have sold out to others and Chet sold his to someone else. Charlie has the home ranch and Andy's son Mike has his father's place. All of the brothers and sisters except Raymond and Andy are still living.

Ernie and Bessie celebrated 55 years of married life before Ernie passed away in December 1974 at the age of 82. Bessie passed away in 1984 at the age of 84. The legacy Ernie and Bessie left was one of great cattle people, farmers, friends, neighbors and parents of 15 children, 52 grandchildren and 64 great grandchildren.

You can truly say that Ernie and Bessie Babcock made their mark at Mud Island in Big Valley.

Glorianne Weigand
August 15, 1993

A Love For Farming

It was the fall of 1914 and Willis and Lydia Joiner were looking for a place of their own to raise alfalfa hay for their dairy cows. They had been living at Pittville in northwest Lassen County and were ready for a change. Their son Albert was five years old and daughter Rose was a small baby. Willis and Albert drove the fifteen Durham milk cows on horse back and Lydia and baby Rose followed behind in the horse drawn wagon. The first night they made it over the hill to the foot of Big Valley mountain. Here they spent the night at the Knochs saw mill, they had to stop to milk the cows. The cows were not used to being milked in an open corral. Willis made a make shift stanchion with rails leaned against a fence to settle the cows so he could milk them. The Joiners then traveled on towards their destination north of Lookout to the Carpenter place that they had bought. On the way they passed by the Louis Kramer Ranch making a shorter route rather than traveling the distance through the Big Valley.

Willis was born in 1875 near Pittville where his dad was a blacksmith. When Willis was old enough he started working on ranches. He had only gone to school a few years which was customary for young boys at that time.

Lydia Brown was born near Dana and went to school in that area. Later she went to the Wilson Preparatory School in Fall River Mills to become a teacher.

Willis Joiner took Lydia Brown as his bride in 1906 at Redding, California. After their marriage they lived at Pittville for a while then moved to a place that they rented from Roderick McArthur for five years before they found the place they decided to buy in Big Valley north of Lookout.

Willis found a good little pony for Albert and he was so proud of it. Willis would never allow his son to ride with a saddle and Albert took many a spill from the back of his little pony. Mr. Joiner had to make trips to Fall River Mills to buy flour and the provisions the family needed. When he returned from one trip, hiding under the seat of the big wagon was a small saddle that was a gift for Albert. A happier boy you never saw.

After moving to Lookout Lydia started her teaching career which lasted for the next thirty years. Where ever Mrs. Joiner taught is where Albert and Rose would go to school. Albert started school at the Butte School between Adin and Lookout. There were mostly Indian children at that school. Then Mrs. Joiner taught at the Craig School in Gougher Neck near the Shaw Ranch. This is where Rose started school. The students at the Craig School decided they wanted to make a reservoir so they would have a skating rink in the winter time. The children worked diligently at recess time building their dam.

Lydia & Willis Joiner.

They hauled rocks and dirt with a wheelbarrow. The boys used their brains while they made the girls use their brawn and the boys hooked the girls to the scoop shovel with a harness and made them pull the shovel. Their little skating rink reservoir held water and made for many hours of fun in the winter time. Today the little reservoir is still there and still holds water.

The little school had a wood cook stove and Mrs. Joiner cooked hot meals for the children.

Albert went to Adin to high school and graduated from there in 1927.

After graduation Albert went to Poly Technique College in Oakland. Then came back to help his dad some and start a ranching and farming career of his own.

Albert started cutting wood for sale and rented some land to farm on his own. A friend that Albert had met when they were young boys came riding into Big Valley on his motorcycle and they decided to go into business together. The friend was Cyril Mamath. Cyril had been in Yuma, Arizona, but always remembered the mountain valley he had visited as a young boy. While in Yuma he got a job and bought a horse and went to Porterville to his uncles truck farm and worked for awhile. Still anxious for the mountains, in 1929 he traded his horse off for a motorcycle and headed to Lookout to look up his old friend Albert Joiner. Albert said Cyril was a dare devil on a motorcycle and would scare Albert to death while he was riding on the back.

The good friends soon decided to go into business together and in 1931 they bought the first John Deere tractor to ever come to Big Valley. They bought the tractor in Alturas and took the lugs off of the steel wheels and drove it to Big Valley. It took them two days to make the trip. They custom farmed for Will Kramer and mowed the swamp for Charlie Gerig and harvested for Charlie also. They hooked two horse mowers together and pulled them with their John Deere. The price for their prize possession was $400.00. They could pull a three bottom plow with their tractor.

During the winter Albert and Cyril would cut wood. They cut all of the wood for the Adin High School. Albert had a one man drag saw and old Model T Ford that they hauled the wood with. They would split and stack all the wood and it took a lot of wood to keep the two story school house warm.

Cyril and Albert bought a second John Deere tractor and a thrashing machine and went into custom farming full time. They would get two thirds of the grain and the owner one third after it was in the bin.

In 1929 Albert met a cute little gal at a dance in Bieber. Her name was Lillian Steiger. Lillian's family had moved around quite a little bit and she had just moved back from Manteca. Lillian's parents Elizabeth and Irvin Steiger had been raised in Big Valley and both of their sons Mellville and Lloyd were born there. Lillian was born in Oakland and the family moved back to Big Valley when she was a young girl. In 1929 Elizabeth and Irvin got a job at the Dixie Valley Ranch. Elizabeth was the cook and Irvin was the chore boy. Lillian had to go to school in Bieber so stayed with Charlie and Elsie Gerig and their daughter Dorotha. A cook's helper was needed at Dixie Valley and Lillian promised her mother the world if she could have the job. Lillian was sixteen and a big help. She said it was such an exciting place to be. At that time Dixie Valley was owned by C.W. Clarke Co. George Retrath was the foreman and a very kind and gentle man. Lillian and her mother cooked for 35 to 40 men every day three meals a day. Everything was cooked from scratch. Breakfast consisted of sourdough biscuits six days a week and sourdough pancakes on Sunday. Fried potatoes, meat and eggs and lots of strong coffee. At the noon meal, pie and pudding was served for dessert and at night, cake and fruit was the dessert. Beans were cooked every day. Every other day bread was baked and every other day than that the butter was churned. There were two dining rooms, the Indian dining room and the cowboy dining room. The Indians did most of the haying with the teams of horses. The winter time cooking was a little easier as there were only fifteen to twenty men to do the winter feeding.

Irvin's job as chore boy was to keep the wood cut for the cook stove and the heating stoves and to keep them going. To milk the cow, cut the meat for every meal, take care of the chickens and do all the chores a woman was not expected to do.

After leaving Dixie Valley the Steigers went to work for Earnest Robinson a neighbor of the Joiners. Later they rented a place in Gougher Neck.

Irvin's mother's family was a Talbot. Along Ash Creek east of Adin was the site of the Talbot barn. It was known as the largest barn ever to be built in Big Valley. It held 400 tons of loose hay and room to tie up over fifty teams of horses. A race track was built around the outside of the barn. Several sheds were on the outside of the barn. A log home stood nearby and the Talbot's home was across the road where the Adin and Lookout road ran through the ranch. The Talbots later took their teams to San Francisco where they supplied teams for the fire department there. Many of their teams were used in the 1906 earthquake.

The Talbot place was sold to the C.W. Clarke Co. Then to the Hunt Estate. The barn started to deteriorate and was torn down and the Hunt Estate used the large timbers to construct dams on their property for irrigation purposes.

Mrs. Steiger worked as a cook for many ranches in Big Valley and Fall River. Some of the ranches she cooked for were Dee Knochs, Hines brothers, Ward Kramer and cared for Nel Vestal. She also was postmaster at Lookout for a few years. Mr. Steiger moved to Burns, Oregon.

After Lillian graduated from Bieber High School in 1931 she went on to nurse's training at Franklin Hospital in San Francisco and became a registered nurse. Albert was still in Big Valley and Lillian came back to the valley and she and Albert were married in Reno, Nevada on his birthday September 5, 1934.

Albert and Lillian moved in with Mr. and Mrs. Joiner for a few years while they had a home built on the ranch. Albert logged the timber and hauled it to the Potter saw mill to be cut into boards. Richard Nichols was the carpenter to build the house and he walked three miles to and from the building site every day and worked for $4.00 a day. Every young couple that were married around lookout, Mr. John Potter gave as a wedding gift a two inch thick twenty-four inch wide clear pine board for a drain board for the new home they would build.

Albert and Lillian moved into their new home in 1936. Albert was still in business with Cyril Mamath and their venture lasted for five years. Cyril then went to work for Will Kramer and married his daughter Katherine in 1936.

The winter of 1936 and 1937 was a hard one with four feet of snow on the level. The feed was not growing in the Red Bluff area and hay had to be hauled by truck from Lookout. There was hay on the Gould Ranch that Metzsker had bought from them, but the snow was so deep the trucks could not get to the ranch. Albert used his RD6 Caterpillar to haul the hay from Gougher Neck to Lookout. He made a sled out of old derrick poles and loaded ten ton of the baled hay onto the sled and towed it to Lookout.

The caterpillar that Albert had bought in 1936 for $3,600.00 Had come in quite handy. He also built a twenty acre reservoir on the Locke place where he kept his cattle in the summer.

The Joiner place was right on Pit River and was the sight of quite a few floods. December 12, 1937 they had one and a half foot of water surrounding their house. In 1962 they flooded again with the equipment under water. Luckily they fed their cattle on the hill above the house and they were safe.

Lillian did not go back to nursing at that time as she was busy being a ranch wife, cooking for hired men, keeping her yard and garden and soon their were children to care for. Their son Bill was born in 1938, Peggy in 1940 and John in 1945.

The winter of 1945 was a wet one and by February the Pit River was roaring and swirling to its full capacity with the melting snow. Willis Joiner had cattle across the river to feed and he used his team with a small cart to cross the ford of the river that they had rocked in. Willis could not swim a stroke, but said he never worried as the horses would take him out of the river if he got into trouble. A young man working for him and Mr. Joiner started to cross the river. He thought it was not that swift. He cut a willow switch to whip the horses across the ford. But the river was more forceful than he thought and washed the horses off of the crossing and tipped the cart over.

Albert & Lillian Joiner.

The team of horses and Mr. Joiner were all drown. When they dragged them from the river Mr. Joiner was clinging to the harness and Albert thought he was trying to cut the horses loose to get them all to safety. The young man with him had been able to swim out.

Albert and Lillian had started to buy several small places to put their ranch together. They had bought 160 acres from a cousin. Then they bought the Locke place, a 160 parcel of B.L.M. land, the Butts and Cooper place they bought from Ernest Robinson. Mr. Robinson wanted cash for his property and Albert went to the Bank of America at Fall River Mills and got $1,000.00 bills to pay him off. Mr. Robinson was so excited as he had never seen so much money. They then bought the Miller place on the east side of the river. All totaled the ranch was 2000 acres.

The Joiners tried several different ventures. They raised cattle and hogs, custom farmed and raised grain, and cabbage. The cabbage grew well, but no market for it in this area. They tried to raise strawberry plants, but their soil was too heavy and clung to the roots. They even tried to wash the plants, but that didn't work. By the time the plants reached San Jose there was no plant life left.

The grange has always been an important part of the Joiner's life. The grange was started by Lydia Joiner in 1925 and she and Willis, Albert and Rose were all charter members. The Lookout grange had 140 members and had a big celebration in June every year. A barbecue, horse show, rodeo and parade were all part of the festivities. Albert was the announcer and master of ceremonies for the big event. A dance was held every Saturday night in the new grange hall they had built in Lookout. Albert and Lillian are both past masters of the grange.

Bill, Peggy and John were all involved in 4-H which was a family affair and kept everyone busy.

After the children grew up Lillian went back to nursing for about ten years and really enjoyed it.

Bill married Barbara Crum from Pittville and they bought part of the ranch from Albert and Lillian and started a home and ranch of their own. They have three children, Dixie, Craig and Jenny.

Peggy married Barbara's cousin, Ted Crum from Pittville and they have two sons, Greg and Duane. They ranch in the Pittville area.

John and his wife Penny live in Eureka, California where he owns an insurance adjusting business. They have two children Joanie and Jason.

In 1969 Albert and Lillian decided it was time to retire. Albert had lived on the ranch for 55 years and Lillian 35 years. They sold the remaining part of the ranch and since that time it has changed hands several times.

The Joiners moved in to the little town of Lookout and have a lovely home there. They have traveled extensively and have been in almost every state in the union and throughout Canada and Mexico.

Albert and Lillian will celebrate their 60th anniversary in September and still love to travel and visit with their friends. Stories could be told for hours about the things they have done and seen. They have a love for life and living and enjoy their family and friends. What a tribute and inspiration they are to the young farmers and ranchers of today.

Glorianne Weigand
May 17, 1994

A Cattleman and a Horse Lover

In the early 1900's Joseph Wayland Stevenson and his wife, Emma, loaded their wagon and headed north from their home in Anderson, California to a new home in Big Valley. Farming, milking cows and raising cattle and horses is how hey made their living. The cattle were mainly Durham and Holstein. When they first came to Big Valley they rented a ranch known as the Kennedy place south of Bieber. Later they rented a place near Pumpkin Center and ranched there for several years. Mr. Stevenson then bought a place at Bieber just north of the cheese factory. Their home stood where the old Standard Oil plant now is and the area that now is part of the town of Bieber was their ranch. This is the reason brother Melvin got the nickname "Cheese" that he was known by his entire lifetime. Living close to the cheese factory was an opportunity for eight year old Melvin to go to the factory and visit. He really loved cheese and he would eat the cheese right out of the tanks. The workers and cheese maker would laugh and say, "Well, here comes Cheesy again", thus the name forever.

The Stevenson family moved closer to the town of Lookout and bought the Arch Eades place. Mr. Stevenson raised many draft horses and the boys would break the Percheron's to ride. The mares were bred to a saddle stallion and the young broke horses were sold to the U.S. Cavalry for remounts. Breaking the horses entertained the rowdy Stevenson boys and made excellent horsemen of them all. These horses were driven to Reno then on to Cottonwood to be sold. At that time everyone used work teams in the Sacramento Valley to farm their row crops with. A good broke team at that time would bring a thousand dollars. All the teams that they sold would have been hooked to the heavy breaking cart and driven before they went to their new owners. The last bunch of horses that were driven out of Big Valley for sale were driven to Anderson by young Joe Stevenson and an Indian girl. Joe cannot remember her name, but said she was quite a cowgirl. She took the lead and the 125 head of horses followed her right over Big Valley Mountain. Joe brought up the tail end of the galloping herd.

Another drive Joe went on taking critters to market was when his dad raised turkeys and they drove hundreds of them to Anderson to market. At sun down you might as well plan on making camp and stop for the evening as the turkeys started to roost in the trees and that was the end of the day's drive.

The children of Joseph and Emma were Wayland, born 1912, Russel (Hap), born 1913, Wanda, born 1914, Melvin (Cheese) born 1916, Winona, born 1919, Jaunita, born 1922, Joe, born 1923, Sam, born 1925 and Nettie, born 1930. All of the children went to school in Bieber. Mr. Stevenson was called into World War I, but he had too many kids and too many cows.

Young Joe said when he was a boy in Big Valley it started to snow the first of November and you never saw the ground until the first of May.

In 1934 the Stevenson cattle had to be driven to where the feed was and they had bought hay at Malin, Oregon, about a sixty-five mile drive. The first day he made it to Monroe Shaw's ranch and spent the night there. They had a big wagon that was pulled by six head of horses breaking trail for the cattle. The snow was so deep the tongue drug in the snow. The small calves were picked up and hauled in the wagon. The cowboys trailed the 300 head of cows for the long cold ride. They wrapped their feet in gunny sacks to keep them from freezing. Joe was only eleven years old, so this was quite an adventure for him. Brother Wayland was the main cowboy and Oscar Scunderson was the main wheel and drove the wagon. Hap, Cheese and Joe were the ramrods. Their dad had to stay home and milk the cows by hand, starting at 3:30 in the morning. Then haul the milk to the cheese factory in Bieber and return in time to start with the evening milking.

The cheese factory sat on the bank of the Pit River at Bieber and that was where all the ranchers would take their milk. After the cheese was made it was put on the railroad and sent all over the world. Wentzell Broadseller was the master cheese maker and he was excellent at his trade. Joe remembers the huge wheels of cheese wrapped in cloth, lining the shelves at the cheese factory. Many hogs were fed on the whey left from the making of the cheese. Babcocks, Stevensons and Bill Harvey were the biggest dairymen in the valley.

The Stevenson cattle were left at Malin for two or three years. Joe grew up working and loving the ranch, all except milking cows. He did his share of the milking but that doesn't mean he liked the chore. The cattle and the horses were Joe's first love and he helped his dad run his cattle on the Indian agency land that he rented between Lookout and Adin. They also had a permit on Fox Mountain on the Forest Service.

Mr. Stevenson did lots of farming and raised lots of grain on land he rented. At harvest time the grain was cut and bound into bundles to be left until a traveling thrasher would come through the valley and thrash everyone's grain. The grain was hauled to Adin to the flour mill and ground into flour. During World War I the government bought every bit of flour that could be produced in Big Valley for the army troops.

When young Joe was seventeen years old he was sent to gather the horses from across Pit River. It was a cold November evening. He was trying to get them to cross the big slough. It was hard for one young lone rider to convince 100 head of horses to cross the icy frozen water. All had crossed but one last horse and he took off. The saddle horse that Joe was riding was ready for the chase, but he fell on the ice and Joe's foot hung up in the stirrup and he was dragged. Finally his foot broke and this gave the opportunity for his boot to come out of the stirrup. When he regained consciousness he realized his leg was so badly broken that the heel was where his toes should be. About ten o'clock that evening his horse went back to the ranch. Cheese and his neighbor and best friend Kim Brown decided they had better go look for Joe. Kim had a Model "A" Ford so they set out to search for Joe. It was 15 degrees above zero and Joe's wet clothes had frozen solid. When Kim and Cheese found him they took him home and taped a board to his leg and hauled him to Adin to Dr. Tinsman. The small town doctor could not help him so they hauled him the forty miles to Alturas to the hospital. Joe spent the rest of the winter in the hospital with a leg that would not heal. Weights were put on the leg to keep it in place. After several weeks a new young doctor had come to Alturas and a new machine had just been purchased, called an x-ray. Joe was the first one to have it used on him. He said it was a small brown box they just set over the leg and took a picture. The x-rays showed the weights were keeping the bones apart and they never would heal in that position. Soon after the weights were removed and a splint was used the leg started to heal.

Joe moved to Lester Babcock's and worked for him milking thirty cows morning and evening to work his way through high school. As bad as Joe hated to milk cows, if this was the only way he could graduate he would do it. Joe graduated from Bieber High School in 1943.

Mr. Stevenson took a logging contract and brother Wayland was sent to work the horses and do the logging for his father. He took an instant liking to the logging industry and thinking it was better than milking cows, he went into that occupation. Young Joe had worked for Homer Jack pitching hay for a dollar a day. While pitching the hay onto the wagons in the field Joe was working with a large man that was stout as a mule. His name was George Bunselmeier and he loved a good joke as well as anyone. Homer had a team of mules that he bragged on constantly that there wasn't a load they couldn't haul. During haying time George was going to prove these mules weren't as good as Homer bragged. Joe was just the driver and would help George load the hay. The nets for the derrick were set on the wagon and George and Joe began to load the wagon. They loaded and loaded and George packed and packed the hay loading the wagon as heavy as he possibly could. George was laughing all the time on the joke he was playing on Homer. Joe drove the team to the stack and they hooked the nets to the mules for them to lift the load to the top of the stack. The mules strained and tugged, but the load would not budge. Homer asked Joe what the problem was. Who loaded the wagon? Joe in his innocence said George and he did. George was out in the field loading another wagon, so Homer sent Joe to unload in the mangers. Joe filled every manger on the ranch and really had to work to pitch the hay that George had packed so hard. George was playing a joke on Homer, but Joe had to pay the price. Joe heard there was a job at the sawmill in Nubieber that paid thirty three cents an hour, but he was too young to work there. He had enough hay pitching. The pay was so much higher he lied about his age and got a job working there for two years.

While Joe was working for Ward Kramer on his ranch he met a young pretty girl from Oklahoma that was working as a clerk at the railroad. Ruby Milliron had gone to a dance and Joe had taken another girl to the dance. After meeting Ruby he let the other girl find another way home and Joe took Ruby home. Six months later on May 27, 1944 Ruby and Joe were married. The going rate for a ranch hand at that time was one hundred twenty five dollars a month.

To supplement their income Joe played in a dance band playing trombone. They called themselves "The Happy Hayseeds." Mr. Stevenson played the violin, sister Nettie played the piano, the cheese maker Wentzell Broadseller played the saxophone and Clyde Gooch played the drums. The singer for the band was Merle Dean Durkee.

Joe and Ruby
before they were married,
1944.

Soon after Ruby and Joe were married the war was getting pretty serious and Joe knew he would soon be drafted, not wanting to go into the army he joined the navy. He was sent to Guam. Joe calls the years he spent in the service the dark horse in his life. While he was overseas, Ruby and baby Larry went back to Oklahoma to spend the time with Ruby's parents.

Joe did some bareback riding in the rodeos for awhile. He said he never had a saddle until he was sixteen, so bareback broncs were quite natural to him.

When Joe was done with his duty they went to Cedarville and went to work for his brother Cheese. A job in Oakdale was available for Dr. Kistler running his 100 cows. Joe took the job and spent thirteen years working there. While there they built the cowherd up to 2000 head and ran 500 head of sheep. The ranch was composed of 9000 acres. 3500 acres was put into production with wells and irrigation. While at Oakdale Joe and Ruby met many rich and famous people. Doctors, lawyers, famous ropiers and movie star Ben Johnson all came to the ranch to hunt pheasant, quail and ducks and eat Ruby's good cooking. This did not phase Joe and Ruby a bit or turn their heads. A good rancher and cattleman is all that Joe wanted to be and he attributes it to a good family and a lot of hard work. Working at Dr. Kistler's was like going to college as he learned so many things.

After Oakdale, Joe was offered more money at Orinda working for Frank Dutra at the feed lot that supplied the meat for the Safeway stores. After several years at the feed lot, Joe's brother Cheese called and told him the John Arreche place was for sale and Joe decided if he was going to work this hard he may as well do it for himself. He bought the 349 acres between Cedarville and Eagleville with the majestic Warner Mountains looking over his land and moved his family back to Surprise Valley around 1960.

Joe and Ruby started their ranch by buying baby calves and raising them on the milk cows and finally got a herd started. Now they run cattle on the Bureau of Land Management and U.S. Forest Service range. One of the cattle ranges at Wall Canyon is fifty miles from the ranch. They drive the cattle and have holding pens every ten miles to corral the cattle for the night. They follow along with the horse trailers to pick up baby calves that tire out on them. Friends and family come to help with the spring cattle drives and branding. The Wall Canyon permit is from the fifteenth of April to the fifteenth of November. The Stevensons did have a good cow camp out there with a good set of corrals and a nice cabin stocked with supplies. Several years ago vandals stole all the boards off of the corrals and barn and ransacked the cabin. Stealing what they could and cutting holes in all the cans of food.

Another one of Joe's permits is at the Triangle Ranch on Devil's Garden near Alturas and the cattle had to be trucked there. Another is a two day drive from the ranch to Long Valley for summer range in Nevada. Joe now runs

Ruby & Joe Stevenson
on their 50th anniversary.

Joe Stevenson carrying the VFW flag.

around 700 head of cows with the help of his son Willie and a couple of hired men.

Two other places were added to the Stevenson Ranch, the Rosendall place then the Kilpatrick place to make the ranch total 945 acres.

Ruby has always been a very important part of the ranch by milking the cows, helping with the farming, doing the books and raising their six children. They are proud that all of their children have gone to college. Larry, Dianne and Linda are all teachers. Jo Ann works for the Forest Service. Laura is an interior decorator and professional country singer and Willie has a hay contracting business and works on the ranch with his father.

All the girls were in the queen contests of the Modoc County Fair all doing very well. Joe and Ruby have been involved for thirty five years in 4-H and FFA. Joe also is active in the VFW and carries the flag every year in the parade as well as supplying most of the horses for the color guard.

The winter of 1993-94 hit the Stevenson Ranch hard with a loss of 146 calves. The usual practice was to calve in January and February. The snow was so deep at one time it took two days to get to the cows through ten foot deep snow drifts. A selenium deficiency was part of the problem with the loss of calves. The cows had no place but a snow bank to lay in for weeks on end. This depleted the protein in their bodies and taking nutrition from the calves and made them weak, they could not survive being born in such severe conditions. Fearing another winter like the last Joe held off a month in turning his bulls out with the cows this year.

While working a heavy cow out of the herd on the ice, Joe's horse fell on him and broke two discs in his lower back. He suffered unbearable pain, but is now back in the saddle again.

Joe sends his weaned calves to a feedlot near Caldwell, Idaho where this year the steers are gaining 3.5 pounds a day and the heifers 2.4. It is costing .46 cents a pound gain and he is planning on selling them by the end of February on the video auction. He likes to send them before it gets too cold in Surprise Valley, so he tries to get them to the feedlot around November 10. At their rate of gain he plans on the steers weighing 800 pounds at sale time.

This is what cattle ranching is all about, loving the land and liking what you are doing and having a good healthy crop of calves to sell at the end of the year.

Joe and Ruby celebrated their 50th wedding anniversary May 27, 1994 and they are still running their ranch and probably will be for some time to come.

Glorianne Weigand
March 1994

The McGarva Clan: Stewards of the Land

From the rugged mountains of Scotland to the meadows, mountains and plains of Modoc County arrived a young Scotsman named Doug McGarva in the fall of 1903. This young adventurer left his home in Girvan, Scotland, to travel to America and left his parents and seven brothers and two sisters behind.

Doug sailed to Montreal, Canada and made his way to San Francisco, traveling mainly by train. He soon found work as a meat cutter for James Allen and Sons. A friend of Mr. Allen, George Bayley, who owned the Corporation Ranch, near Likely in Modoc County had bought a herd of cattle and needed someone to feed them, and a chore boy on his ranch. Doug was more of a country boy than a city boy and he felt this was a great opportunity for him. His family had been sheepherders in Scotland and ran their own sheep as well as sheep for other people.

By 1906 Doug was getting homesick for his family so he returned to Scotland for a visit and take Margaret Rae as his bride. The newlyweds and Doug's brothers John and Jimmy set sail for America.

In 1908 three other members of the family followed their brothers to the promised land of opportunity. The stipulation at the time was that you had $100.00 in your pocket to enter America and clear customs. Two brothers, Ivie and Robert, and sister Lizzie only had $100.00 between them. One of them would pass through the line and hand the money on to the second one and then on to the third one until they had all shown the same $100.00.

The McGarva parents, Robert and Isabelle, and three sons, Peter, Anthony and Ronald and daughter Jessie were still in Scotland. All the members of the family in America worked and saved their money to bring the rest of the family over to be with them. When enough money was raised by 1912, the family tried to get tickets on the Titanic, but the huge and famous ship was already over-booked. Disappointed, they made arrangements to sail on the Titanic's sister ship. It was a month before their ship set sail. They were so thankful they were unable to sail on the Titanic. Everyone was edgy because of the destiny of the ill-fated ship and were on the lookout for

Heading cattle to the range for the summer by Duane McGarva.

icebergs. Early one evening on their voyage the passengers thought they saw an iceberg looming in their path. The passengers were frantic and screamed for the captain to change their course. At that time what they thought was an iceberg suddenly turned out to be another ship that had not yet turned on their lights.

In 1907 when John McGarva landed in America, he only had ten dollars in his pocket and the clothes on his back. When Pete came to the west, his first job was in Lovelock, Nevada, feeding cattle. He then came to the Likely country and worked for other cattlemen and ran sheep on shares.

Ivie, John, Jim and Pete became partners in the sheep business. They had what was known as the Ivie McGarva Ranch at the south end of South Fork Valley. After several years, Ivie and Jim withdrew from the partnership and Peter and John, known as Jake, went on with their ranching venture. In the beginning, the family from Scotland ran only shorthorn cattle. Since that time they have evolved into hereford cattle.

In 1914, two years after Pete had come to America, he and John bought what was known as the Blue Lake Ranch from Miles and Ed Sigler. The ranch was situated in the Warner Mountains, near Jess Valley. The ranch consisted of 650 acres of meadow and they could put up enough hay to winter their cattle there.

By 1919 John and Peter thought it was time to expand so they bought another ranch from Frank McArthur, who owned the Corporation Ranch near Likely. This was to be the home ranch and main headquarters of the McGarva clan from Scotland for generations to come. The original ranch was 210 acres of meadow and 90 acres on the hill. The water was plentiful and the meadows were lush.

Doug McGarva had helped to dig the west side canal to drain the swamps to make the meadows. They used twenty horse teams with an excavator to do the tremendous task. In the early 1940's the canal was widened with drag lines.

By 1925, the Forest Service and the Bureau of Land Management had started to fence their properties. The cattle were no longer left to roam as they pleased. By 1933, the Taylor Grazing Act was adopted to keep transient stock from wandering the ranges. This kept the people that were not land owners or owned ranches in the area from grazing without a right. The amount you were allowed to run was figured on the capacity of the home ranch. Pete and John were running around 700 cows with the Blue Lake Ranch and the Likely Ranch, so they were granted a range permit for that many cattle.

At that time the end of the NCO railroad was at Madeline. This was only a few miles away and this was the largest sheep shipping station in the United States. This caused a problem with the stockmen in the Likely area as thousands of sheep were driven from all of Oregon and Idaho through the range country and farm land of Likely on their way to load on to the train for their trip to market. The sheep herders let their bands of sheep graze along the way and they devastated some of the rangelands in that area.

Pete met a pretty young girl at a bull sale in 1927 and on New Year's Day in 1928, Pete and Phyllis Rogers were married. Pete was thirty years old and Phyllis was only seventeen. Phyllis had been born at Camp Rogers, a recreational camp in the Feather River Canyon, and was raised in Oakland, California. Her parents died when she was thirteen and she lived in Oakland for another year. Her aunt and uncle, Anne and Bert Bath, lived near Adin, California. Phyllis was sent to live with these relatives. She had to travel by herself on the Western Pacific train to Amity, where she spent the night at the Amity Hotel. Then she boarded the Nevada, California, Oregon train to Madeline, where her Uncle Bert picked her up. She went to school in Adin and graduated from high school there.

After Pete and Phyllis were married, they moved to the ranch at Likely. A new home was constructed that was a pre-cut house from the east. It was delivered on the railroad to Bayley Siding, near Likely.

Summers were spent at the Blue Lake Ranch, where there was a two story log home in the middle of the meadow. The Blue Lake Ranch was sold to the Forest Service in 1946 after the Forest Service told the McGarva's that if a fire started on their ranch and spread into the surrounding forest that the McGarvas would be responsible. The Forest Service then burned the log home down.

In the fall of 1938 Peter and John sold cows for two cents a pound. This was not a lot of money, but to make matters worse, when Peter took the check to the Modoc Bank in Alturas he deposited it and walked out the door. The door was locked behind him and the bank had gone out of business. With some luck he was able to get his money back the next day.

In 1935, Phyllis and Peter started their family when their first son Duane was born. In 1938, a brother Kenneth, was welcomed into the family. This was the beginning of the partnership that still stands strong in the cattle business today.

In 1957, John and his wife Maude, decided to retire and move to town. This was an opportunity for Peter's sons to go into business with him. At this time Peter bought his brother John out.

Duane and Kenneth both went to the schools at Likely and Alturas. They both went to the University of California at Davis to study agriculture.

Duane married Dixie Welch in 1958 and was drafted into the army that same year. Duane was sent to Germany and Dixie followed him. After Duane was discharged from the service, they returned to Likely to the ranch. They have three children, Lynne, Scott and Aimee.

Tim Lanham, Duane McGarva, Kenneth McGarva, Shane McGarva, Lester Porter, Jason Schuh.

In 1958, Kenneth and Jackie Haise were also married. They moved to the ranch and went to work for Peter. Kenneth and Jackie have three children, Ross, Shane and Rhonda.

In 1968 Duane and Kenneth bought their parents out and Peter and Phyllis moved to Alturas to retire. They celebrated their 50th wedding anniversary in 1978 on New Year's Day and Phyllis passed away that August. Peter passed away in 1981.

The brothers bought the Gaustad Ranch and in 1973 Kenneth and Duane bought out a neighboring ranch of Nelson Monroe. This added one thousand acres on the east side of their home ranch and enabled the McGarva's to run 1100 head of cattle. In 1989, five hundred more acres known as the Beet Camp was added to their holdings. When this property was owned by the Corporation Ranch, sugar beets were raised on it and that is why it was called the Beet Camp.

The McGarva brothers are known as some of the best stewards of the land in Modoc County. They manage their cattle and public range lands as well as any rancher around. Changes on the range have been made by a 70% cut on their BLM grazing land. Over a period of years they were cut from three hundred and five head to one hundred and sixty-eight head, then cut again to sixty four head. After that they took a 30% voluntary cut for range betterment. The biggest cause of this range grazing reduction is because of the juniper

Peter & Matthew Heryford, Lynne (McGarva) Heryford's sons.

encroachment. In a picture taken in 1916 compared to the picture of the same area in 1983, it is well documented how the juniper have taken over the range lands.

It is proven by cutting juniper trees around a spring area, the capacity flow of the spring was doubled overnight. It is known that a juniper tree will consume 250-300 gallons of water per day. So no wonder springs dry up and grass is depleted in the juniper populated areas.

In the Cedar Creek Riparian Restoration Project, the McGarva allotment was cut by 50%. This is to be reinstated in the near future.

Prescribed burns on the BLM in 1990 were implemented and then the range was given a two year rest. It was then used in the fall of 1992 and the summer of 1993. Another prescribed burn was the Meeks Canyon, east of Madeline, where they burned 1200 acres. Another 3000 acres was burned at Dead Horse Flat in 1991. These burns have improved the range and forage a great deal and has eliminated a lot of the competitive vegetation.

In Clark's Valley the McGarva's and the BLM put in seventeen miles of fence so cattle could be controlled in Riparian areas. The pasture in the Riparian area is large enough so they can graze the pasture for a short duration. Their Forest Service permits are stable and they graze from May 1 to September 30.

Cattle are driven home from the range, a distance of twenty-two miles. This is a two day drive. The cattle are herded from Blue Lake to Likely the first day and then driven on to the home ranch the next day. Some of the cattle that are on a range thirty miles away are trucked.

Cattle are kept at the home ranch all winter and are fed the 2500 tons of hay that has been put up on the meadows during the summer by Duane, Kenneth and his son Shane, and three or four hired men that they employ year around.

Water is abundant on the McGarva Ranch with the meadows being irrigated from the Pit River, West Valley Reservoir, and the West Side Canal, and the East Side Canal.

At branding time friends and neighbors all come to help and they usually have six ropers at a time. Young and old alike get in on the busy event.

Cattle are marketed through cattle buyers and the local auction yards. In recent years like many other ranchers, the McGarva brothers have been selling some of their cattle on the video satellite auction.

Kenneth and Duane are both very active in community affairs. The brothers were both recognized as cattlemen of the year for the Modoc County Cattlemen in 1985.

Duane has been director of the Surprise Valley Electrification Corporation for twenty years, past president of the Modoc County Cattlemen and is currently president of the Modoc County Historical Society.

(Left to right) Peter McGarva, his wife Phyllis (Rodgers) and older brother John McGarva (known as Jake). Photo taken on the front porch of the family home at the Blue Lake Ranch, Lassen County, in the summer of 1930.

Kenneth is chairman of the BLM grazing board, president of the irrigation district, director of the Modoc County Cattlemen, past president of Modoc County Cattlemen and commissioner of the fire district.

Both brothers have been instrumental in the 4-H organization of the county and are very supportive of the local junior livestock show.

The day that the McGarva family decided to leave Scotland for America, the land of opportunity, was truly a day the cattle industry and the county of Modoc were blessed with true stewards of the land, Duane and Kenneth McGarva.

Glorianne Weigand
November 15, 1993

Louis Kramer Began Ranching Legacy In Big Valley

George Louis Kramer was born in Girkhousen, Germany in 1850. In 1879 when he was 29 years old he decided to fulfill a lifetime dream and leave his family and travel to America. The Kramer family had a guest house to run in the old country and this was not the ambition of this young man.

The ship that brought him to the new world docked at New York and Louis, now being known as Louie soon joined up with an emigrant train traveling to the wild west. The destination of his wagon train travels brought him to Fall River Mills, California. He had cousins there that owned the Florin Brothers Flour Mill and Saw Mill. Louie went to work for his cousins for a time.

While in Fall River Valley Louie was broke, down to his last dime. He vowed never to spend the dime and he carried it in his purse until his death. The engraving was worn completely off and it was smooth and paper thin, but it was an omen and a good luck piece for the young man from Germany.

Also while in the Fall River Valley Louie worked on the Jackson Toll Road now known as Hatchet Mountain. He collected the toll and tried to keep the road passable with a pick and shovel. That same year of 1883, Will Kramer, Louie's brother came from Germany to join him.

When Louie decided it was time to move on he came over the hill into Big Valley and went to work for Mr. Powers on his ranch. After working for some time, there was no money to pay the hired help so in lieu of pay they gave Louie a piece of land. The first deed was recorded on July 27, 1885 from Lewis Powers and E. Florin to Louis Kramer. He began his life as a renowned cattle rancher with 160 acres, 3 horses and 5 head of cattle.

The homestead he had acquired was one of the first in Big Valley, settled by Thomas Turnbull in 1868. The cabin on his property was the first cabin built in the valley.

Winters were hard in the mountains of Lassen and Modoc Counties and soon homesteaders were wanting to move on to a better climate. Many that were neighbors of Louie sold out to him and moved on. Eventually he had purchased the holdings of eleven other homesteaders.

The nearest railroad to ship cattle to market in the early days was Marysville, California. Louie, like many other ranchers of that time had to make the long drive which was a month long trip. Louie would take some of his neighbor's cattle along with him on this journey.

Louie registered the 12 bar brand on the right rib in 1890 and it is still used to the present time by his grandson Charles Kramer.

In February of 1890 the grass was green and had grown due to a mild winter, but on March 28 it started to snow and was the hardest snowfall of the winter. Many ranchers were low on hay so they turned their cattle out to

Carrie Kresge and Louis Kramer, wedding picture 1903.

graze the grasslands. The cattlemen could not get feed to their cattle and the snow was too deep to drive the cattle to feed so many cattle were lost. It has been said you can survive the winters in Big Valley, it is the spring you have to be wary of.

One of the homesteads that was purchased by Louie was the Carmichael place which was the first sawmill in Big Valley. It was run by water power and the old saw went up and down. This is now the present site of the reservoir that helps supply the irrigation water for the Kramer Ranch.

An article in the *Adin Argus Gazette* on June 3, 1903 stated that Louis Kramer and Carrie Kresge from Gougersneck, near Lookout were married at the City Hotel in Adin. Both contracting parties are well known in this valley and highly respected for their sterling qualities. Reverend Harry Perks officiated and witnesses were brother of the bride Seward Kresge and hotel proprietress Mrs. Harry Williams. The marriage license states the husband is the head of the house, and the wife is the crown of the husband.

Carrie had been a teacher at the Pleasant District School. The new bride was not new to the ranch life as her own family had come to Big Valley and homesteaded in Gougersneck in 1877 when she was only three years old. Carrie was born in Straudsburg, Pennsylvania in 1873 and came across the plains by train with her family.

Louie and Carrie ran a large ranch with many hired hands for Carrie to cook for. In 1904 their son, Ward, was born and in 1908 a daughter, Orma, was born.

In 1904 Louie bought about 2500 acres of land from the government for less than $1.00 an acre. This is known as Egg Lake and used for summer pasture. To this he added three homesteads, the Knoch, Harris and the Huffman farms. The stipulation on the government land was that it had to have the land reclaimed from the swamps. It took two years to build the levy to control the water. It took five teams of horses to pull the excavator to build the levy.

This portion of the ranch was so close to the lava beds that the rattlesnakes were a real problem. George Kresge lived at Egg Lake and raised grain. The grain grew tall and beautiful. The heads would form, but no grain would fill the heads, so the crop was useless. To control the rattlesnakes George would let his hogs run free near the house to kill the snakes.

Little Egg Lake was added to the property until today the Egg Lake property is around 5000 acres. This is the summer pasture of the Kramer cattle along with a very small Forest Service and Bureau of Land Management permit.

In 1909 during haying season the Kramer cabin caught fire and burned. The hay crew were coming in from the field and one of the men ran in and grabbed Orma who was sitting in her high chair and took her, chair and all

40

Building the levy at Egg Lake.

out to the yard safe from the fire. Carrie, a frantic mother could not find her child. She was much relieved when she saw Orma happily sitting in her chair out under the trees. The large home that stands today was built in 1909, by George and John Kresge.

The Kramer Ranch raised many horses and mules. They were mainly used for putting up their own hay. They needed thirty or more horses for this job. Horses and mules were also rented out to build the Said Valley Reservoir, county roads and to neighbors. Most of the time one of the hired hands would go to work the teams so they would be sure they would be well taken care of.

To feed all the hay crew in the summer, a cook house was built on wheels to be pulled to the fields by horses. It was stationed in three different locations during the summer. The cook at that time was Mrs. Elliott. After the cookhouse was built at the ranch the men were taken to the fields in a truck and brought in to the cook house at noon, leaving the horses in the field to rest at the meal time, then brought back for the evening.

Even after Louie was letting the reins of the ranch be held by Ward, he kept very active. He would drive his horse and cart around the ranch and tend to the water. His old buggy horse named Sleepy would pull the buggy from place to place and stand patiently and wait for Louie to check his water and soon Sleepy would get bored and tired and turn the shaves of the buggy from side to side telling his partner it was time to go home. Louie carried a Big Willow switch that reminded Sleepy he was still the boss.

In 1933 Ward married Dorotha Gerig who was also born in Big Valley. Her family were pioneers of the valley and her father Charles Gerig was also a rancher. Dorotha and Ward moved into the large ranch home with Mr. and Mrs. Kramer. The elder Kramers had planned on moving to Adin and letting the newlyweds have the ranch home. But Louie Kramer became ill and unable to move. He passed away August 14, 1934. Carrie Kramer stayed on with Ward and Dorotha for a time, then went to stay with Orma and Ed in Oregon when Dale was born. Carrie lived most of her remaining years with the Albaughs, but was at the ranch where she came as a bride with Ward and Dorotha when she passed away April 14, 1968. Carrie had cherished the honor bestowed upon her when she was named Cowbelle Mom of the Year in 1962 by the Inter-Mountain Cowbelles.

In 1934 Orma married Ed Albaugh. They moved to Baker, Oregon where Ed was an emergency AG assistant. They have three children Dale, Jean and Ron. Ed and Orma now run the Frosty Acres Ranch in Adin with their sons Dale and Ron.

Ward and Dorotha started their family and in 1935 their daughter Mardell was born and in 1938 their son Charles was born. Many other young men and women came to call the Kramer Ranch their home as the big house always

Carrie, Orma, Louis and Ward Kramer.

42

had room for one more child that needed a home or loving care. There was always a welcome mat out for those that needed a place to stay or work.

In 1933 a new cook house was built and the horse drawn cook house was put to rest for a play house for the children. The men were taken to the hay field in the morning in a truck and brought back for the noon meal and again at night. Twenty to twenty-five men were fed their meals there for three months out of the year. The hay crew was four teams for mowing, three teams to rake, four teams for wagons and a derrick team. The same men came to help each year. The first baling of hay was done by Otis Leonard in 1942.

The Northwestern Railroad came into Big Valley in 1931. The route it chose was the full length of the Kramer property, dissecting the ranch through the meadows. A livestock loading facility was located within a short distance from the ranch. Although Louie did not enjoy the thought of having the intruder going through his property he did like the idea of being able to ship his cattle without driving them for days.

In 1933 a large reservoir was also built on the old Carmichael Mill site and the Vickers place. The reservoir was fed by many small warm springs and as people would swim they could feel the flow of warm water. The dam washed out and had to be rebuilt in 1972.

In 1936 a slaughter house was built to accommodate the twenty or more hogs that were butchered each year and the many beef it took to feed the large crew.

Three of the young people that called the Kramer Ranch their home were Buster Bouse, Marion Carmichael and Louise Bouse. Louise came to live with the Kramers when she was nine years old.

Buster Bouse came to work in 1937 when he was fourteen years old and worked the summers until he went into the war. After he returned from the service he married Ruth Babcock in 1948 and they moved into a home on the ranch. Buster and Ruth worked on the ranch for forty-six years and raised their children Dan, Dorothy and Jean there.

Buster retired and moved to Adin but still feels very much a part of the family and heritage of the Kramer Ranch.

Buster's brother, Henry, also worked on the ranch and along with Marion that made three servicemen from the Kramer Ranch all at one time to serve in World War II.

Marion Carmichael, known as Mike, started walking a few miles each day from his home when he was around ten years old to follow his idol, Ward Kramer in his daily tasks. When Charles was born Mike would watch the baby while Dorotha did her work. Ward started giving Mike some chores of packing the wood, taking care of the chickens and any small job the young lad could do. Mike was always eager and willing just to be part of the crew. Ward would pay him a few dollars now and then, but Mike would have happily

Dorothy and Ward Kramer, 1963.

done the work for nothing. In 1939 Mike became a part of the Kramer hay crew and worked until he also was called into the service. When he returned he married Bunny Steele in 1949 and they made their home on the ranch, raising their two daughters June and Connie.

Mike stayed on the ranch for twenty-five years then left for another job and then on to work for the Forest Service as a range technician in Adin. He passed away in 1993.

A registered herd of horned herefords were started by Ward and some bulls were sold to other ranchers. In 1961 Ward received a large trophy from the Modoc County Cattlemen at the Modoc County Fair for the champion range bull. Today a small herd of the registered cattle are still kept on the ranch, but only to raise some of the fifty bulls needed to breed their own cows.

There were always busy times on the Kramer Ranch and happy times, but also sad times invaded them. On August 21, 1972 Ward and some neighbors were working cattle. The ranch meadow is full of meandering sloughs and channels of the Pit River. As Ward attempted to cross one of the sloughs his horse could not climb the slick bank and fell backwards with him and Ward drowned. This kind and loving man was doing one of the things he loved most, riding his horse and working cattle.

Dorotha and Charles were left to run the ranch, and were thankful for the capable help of the men that had worked for them for years.

Charles built a home on the hill overlooking the ranch. He loved the rodeo life and especially the roping events. While at one of the rodeos he met a young barrel racer, Karen Hale and on October 26, 1963 they were married. In 1966 a son Randy was born and in 1972 another son Rob was born.

Dorotha, Charles and Karen went on to carry on the Ward Kramer estate and run it as it had been for the past generations. Dorotha still lives in the large ranch home and keeps an interest as to what is going on at the ranch. Dorotha also was very instrumental in the beginning of the senior citizens program and in starting the museum in Bieber. People who know Dorotha well say she should have been a nurse as she was always there to help the sick or elderly when there was a need.

Daughter Mardell and her two sons, Steven and Jay Dunlap are frequent visitors to the ranch.

Charles and Karen were both involved in 4-H and FFA with their sons as most ranch parents are. Rodeos and roping events are still enjoyed by all the family. Randy and his wife Robin and Rob still live on the ranch and enjoy the huge brandings and get togethers while working cattle. Karen's love is team penning and she has scored high in that competition and was invited to the finals at Carson City, Nevada. Charles enjoys the roping events more.

April 1, 1982 made all ranchers in Big Valley prove themselves. It is said that history repeats itself, and as with the heavy snow of March 28, 1890, another freak storm hit the valley in 1982. Four feet of snow came so fast and in the height of calving season. Cows calving melted down into the snow and could not get up, the baby calves were buried in the white depths of the blinding snow to be smothered, or froze to death. Even making a feed bed with a caterpillar was to no avail and moving the cattle to the timber for protection caused the cows to eat the pine needles and abort their calves. An excess of 100 calves were lost in a matter of hours. The Kramers were not alone as the same tragedy hit all of the ranchers.

Cattle are summered in the hills and at Egg Lake then returned to the meadows in the fall until feeding time. About two hundred and fifty cows are hauled to Anderson, California for winter pasture and to calve out. The rest are left at home and all the heifers are calved at the ranch. A strong vaccination program is faithfully followed and true herdsmanship is practiced.

Longhorn bulls are used to breed the heifers. Angus and Saler bulls are used for the second calf cows, and Hereford bulls are used to breed the older cows.

Marketing cattle is different today than the days of driving them for days to market. Satellite video auction has come to be an important part of selling the Kramer cattle or they sell them at the Shasta livestock market. The cattle buyers that used to travel the valley in the fall are almost a thing of the past.

Every cattle rancher knows there are truly four seasons in this old world. Calving season, haying season, gathering and branding season and feeding season. No one has us fooled, that is if you are one of the lucky ones to call Big Valley home.

Glorianne Weigand
November 15, 1993

The Crum Meat Company 1932-1971

It was during the depression. There were no jobs to be had. Merton Crum had some hogs that needed to be sold and he couldn't sell them. He told his son Donald if he would drive him around Fall River Valley that he would butcher the hogs and they would try to sell the meat. They peddled the meat from house to house and made three times as much money as Merton would have if he had sold the live hogs by the pound. Merton and his father had butchered and sold meat in Dana years earlier. You might say that this was the beginning of the Crum Meat Company that was to become a very important enterprise in the Fall River Valley in years to come. Even though it did not get its official start until 1932.

Merton Crum was born in Honey Lake Valley near Susanville, California, January 1874. He had moved to the Fall River Valley area in northeastern California and married Bertie Rogers from Dana in 1901.

The Crum's lived at Dana for a time then they decided to move to Burns, Oregon. Bertie drove one wagon and Merton drove the other and they made the long trip. After two years they decided to return and they and their two small children, Jim and Harold again hitched up their wagons and headed back to northern California settling in Cayton Valley. In 1920 they moved to the McArthur area and took up their third homestead and this is where they stayed and raised their family of nine children. There on the banks of the Pit River they built their home, started their ranch and built a very small slaughter house.

The Crum children, Jim, Harold, Jack, Blanch, Orville, Hiram, Nelda, Allan and Donald all walked a mile and a half to attend the Beaver Creek School. Sometimes the snow was mighty deep and it could be very cold. There were thirty-seven students in one room with one teacher and all eight grades. The Crum, Ingram, Bruce, Dawson, Knoch and Bean children were some of the families that went to school there and drank their water from and played in Peacock Creek.

The older Crum boys grew up and Jim started to peddle the meat that his father butchered in the little slaughter house on the ranch. They butchered in

Bertie Rogers & Merton Crum, wedding picture 1901.

one end and hung it in the other end. Jim only had a little Ford coupe that he used to peddle meat. The business began to grow as everyone was anxious for the fresh meat the Crums had to offer. Orville and Harold and Allan were doing the butchering. The ranch also had to be kept running and it was a big job and everyone did their share of the work.

Young Jack was very sick and took constant care from their mother Bertie. She held him so much to comfort him that it caused her to lose the use of her arm. Jack died when he was thirteen years old. Bertie was a wonderful mother and raised nine children in seventeen years. A hard worker and a wonderful mother who passed away at the age of 54.

Being left with a home full of hungry children, Mr. Crum had to hire cooks to do that chore. There were sometimes eighteen men to cook for. There was the hay crew and the butchering crew was getting larger as the Crum Meat Company was growing. There was also the family itself.

The Crum Meat Company was established and Jim and Harold built a new slaughter house on the ranch in 1932. This one replaced the one that Merton had first built. Orville and Harold did the butchering and Allan delivered the meat.

Jim had moved over the hill to Nubieber and started a butcher shop there.

The meat was peddled in a little van that Allan could put a 150 pound block of ice in the center and keep the meat cool. His route took him to the lumber camps of Pondosa, McCloud and White Horse. As he would pull into Pondosa to peddle from door to door women would run to his van and as many as eight at a time would stand in line anxious to have fresh meat. They would either pay at the time or Allan would write it down using the walls of his truck for his place to figure. When he would get back to the meat company in McArthur Hiram who was the bookkeeper would have to decipher his scribbling on a piece of paper or the truck wall so he would know who to charge. Some ladies paid cash, others paid at pay day and some never paid at all.

The request for chickens and fresh eggs started to come in so this was added to the growing inventory of fresh beef, and pork. Cured ham, and bacon, sausage and wieners. Donald can remember picking chickens in the morning before he went to school so there would be fresh chickens for his brother to deliver.

The Crum boys put in a store in McArthur to sell their meat products. Hiram took care of the meat market with the help of the other brothers cutting and wrapping the meat. Hiram was the bookkeeper as he had gone to business college in Sacramento.

This is a unique family as the one small 160 acre homestead of Bertie and Merton Crum was making a living for six families. Merton had bought more land and enlarged the ranch but the slaughter house and the meat company was the main part of their income. It was during the depression when so many were out of jobs, but the hard-working Crum brothers never lacked for a job.

In back: Jim & Harold.
In front: Bertie, Orville, Donald, Blanch, Nelda, Hiram, Allan, and Merton.

The slaughter house was butchering two to three days a week and doing 40 to 60 beef a day and 40 to 60 hogs. This was only their commercial slaughtering. They also did custom butchering that was another 15 beef and 15 hogs a week for the local ranchers. They also butchered lambs.

When the slaughter house first started operating they had no electricity and had to do everything by hand. They were lucky for the fact that they had a wonderful Artesian well for their water supply for the slaughter house and the family homes.

The little van that Allan drove soon was not big enough to take care of the amount of meat they were selling. They bought a ton and a half truck and their delivery area was growing rapidly.

The demand for the fresh meat from the meat company and their wonderful hams and bacons was known far and wide. The delivery area included the P.G.& E. Camps, McCloud, Pondosa, Mt. Shasta, Fall River area, Burney, Redding, Big Valley, Alturas, Cedarville, Susanville and all points in between. What started out as a small trip to sell a few butchered hogs was a booming business.

Harold also started to run the meat truck and he was doing the buying from local ranchers to stock the Crum feed lots to fatten out the cattle. Donald soon started doing some of the buying also.

The Crums had 20 to 30 sows to raise their own pigs for the meat company, but also bought feeder pigs or fat hogs from ranchers. They had 700 to 800 cattle in their feed lot to fatten for the slaughter plant. They also had their own cow herd, but bought many from local ranchers also. They

The Crum slaughter house in its heyday.

50

raised quite a bit of their own feed for the stock, but not near enough for the amount they had to feed. They bought a lot of grain from Big Valley farmers Albert Joiner and Kim Brown. They also had it shipped in by train to Nubieber on the railroad and had to truck it over Big Valley Mountain to their feedlots.

The government inspection was started and the Crums had to rebuild the slaughter house to meet the state requirements. A government meat inspector was an addition to the Crum Meat Company and Dr. Wilmont and Dr. Don Gomez were the meat inspectors. Evan Guttry was a long time brand inspector at the Crum Meat Company.

The state inspectors were easy to work with and things went well with the Crum Meat Company. Soon the federal government decided they wanted to be included in the inspection process and it made it harder to keep up with all the rules and regulations.

The present slaughter house did not meet all the government requirements so a third slaughter house was built to their specifications.

The Crum Meat Company was known for their wonderful hams and bacons. The procedure to process a hog was to kill it, scald it and scrape all the hair off. In two or three days the fresh meat could be sold. The bacon was done by dry curing. Curing salt and sugar were mixed and rubbed into the sides of bacon. Layering the slabs of bacon, one on another. They were left to cure for a week then put in the smoke house for a day to dry and smoke.

The hams were put into a salt brine to soak for three weeks. The brine would be injected into the fleshy part of the ham with a special injection gun to cure it near the bone. After the brine bath the hams were washed in cold water to get the salt off then smoked in the smoke house. Oak and mahogany wood were the favorites to use in the smoke house. The government regulations made them get the hams to a certain temperature and one time they almost cooked them before they got that process down to a technique.

Nothing was wasted at the slaughter house. The offal from the butchering was cooked in a huge steamer and the tallow was drained off to sell to a tallow factory or saw mills to grease their wheels and gears. The cooked offal was mixed with the grain and fed to the hogs to fatten them. The proper intestines were cleaned and scraped for the casings for the wieners, sausages and bologna. The wieners and sausage were stuffed, twisting or tieing in between each link. The wieners and bologna were then cooked and smoked. The heads from the animals were skinned completely out and all the meat was used. The head of a beef would supply up to eight pounds of hamburger.

Delivering meat was not always the easy part of the job. Like the mail it is said must go through, the meat must go through. Flood, snow, wind or whatever. People had to eat. One time when Allan was delivering meat to Pondosa the snow was so deep he couldn't get through. He then heard that they had taken a caterpillar out with a sled on it and had made a track. He thought his light little truck might make it on top of the sled tracks. It didn't hold his vehicle up and he broke through and was stuck. While he waited for help to come he decided to check how deep the snow was and dug five feet before he hit the road bed.

When meat had to be delivered during a flooding time to White Horse Lumber Company the swollen creek could not be crossed. The Crum brothers had to park on one side while the lumber company had a truck on the other side and they had to wade the swollen waters waste deep with a quarter of beef on their back to deliver the meat.

The Crum brothers started to think about getting married and started to choose their lifetime partners.

Jim married Rachel Gouchman and they had one daughter Dorothy. Harold married Louise Gilmore and they have two children Lucille and Merton.

Orville married Alice Wendt and they have two children Muriel and Bill. Blanch married Orie Anders and they have two children Ronald and Marjorie. Nelda married Herman Taylor and they had two sons Jack and Norman. Hiram married Ersel Wendt and they had two sons John and Jim. Allan married Esther Hobson and they had five children, Beverly, Barbara, Melvin, Ida Marie and Don. Donald married Irene Nye and they have two children, Ted and Helen.

All the wives worked along with their husbands on the ranch and in the meat company. Alice cooked most of the breakfasts, Louise, Ersel, Irene and Esther cooked the other meals. At times there were up to eighteen men to cook for. Besides the butchering crew there was the hay crew and one year the Schneider men were building barns on the ranch and ate with the Crum crew. The laundry was a big chore and besides the clothing that had to be washed, the shrouds for the meat had to be washed. Before there were wives to do the laundry the boys would haul the laundry to their sister Nelda in Burney to do.

The wives would help with the meat wrapping and anything else they could do to be included in the family business.

Many cooks came and went for the Crum Company and one of their best was Annie Farrell. She cooked there for many years. A lot of the cooks would stay through the winter when there were not so many to cook for, but when the crew increased in the summer they would leave and the Crum women would have to fill in to feed the hungry hands.

A lot of the hay crew they hired in the summer were young rowdy boys that liked to have a little fun. One of the cooks told Donald to fire those sassy boys. Donald informed the cook he hired her to cook for those boys. He didn't hire the boys to eat her cooking. She was soon on the way out the door.

The Crum Family.
Back: Hiram, Jim, Don & Allan. Front: Harold, Blanch, Nelda & Orville.

Many different men came and went at the slaughter plant. Paul Dawson worked for many years for the Crums. One night he went to check the boiler late in the evening. Just before he got there the boiler blew up and went through the wall and the tank still lays in the field where it landed. Another time when Orville was checking the boiler all the steam was not released and when it was opened it burned Orville severely.

A neighbor, Al Bruce, helped to butcher and scrape hogs. Al had his own ranch to run and stock to feed so he only worked there on butchering days.

On one of the trips from Redding that Allan had taken to deliver meat he hit a deer on the way home. He hit the buck in the head with his truck. As he backed up the horns of the deer got hung up under the bumper. Allan got out and cut the deer's throat and threw him into the back of the meat truck. It was during deer season so he put his deer tags on him. When he got to the butcher shop in McArthur he opened the door to drag the buck into the shop and the deer jumped up and about ran through the big front window. Allan and a young man had to tackle him down and this time Allan was sure he did a little better job with his knife. The next morning when Donald and Harold arrived they were baffled not to find a bullet hole in the buck.

Some of the Crum brothers started to venture out on their own. Allan sold out to his brothers in 1944 and started ranching on his own. He did help some still on butchering days. Allan was raising hogs and had a load to take to the slaughter plant on the day they were to be butchered. He had a stake side truck and had quite a few hogs on the load. As he was driving down the road past the Bruce Ranch he did not notice that someone had run into the phone line and it was hanging low across the road. The racks of the truck hung up on the phone line and it pulled them off. A few hogs fell off the truck at the time, but the rest of them rode the flat bed truck to the slaughter plant and waited for Allan to back up to the unloading ramp. The ones that fell off had to be driven a mile and a half.

Jack and Norman Taylor, nephews of the Crum brothers started working on the ranch when they were around eleven years old. When they were fourteen they started helping in the slaughter house with general work.

Donald sold out in 1953 and he and Irene bought a ranch near Pitville. Orville also bought a ranch in 1958 when Jack and Norman Taylor bought him out. Harold later also sold out to the Taylor brothers, Hiram and Paul Dawson.

Norman was now the main cow buyer. Jack and Paul were at the plant and Hiram ran the meat market in town. Norman was delivering meat to Redding and on one of the trips the snow was so bad he had to put chains on seven times for the round trip.

Norman's wife Betty, and Jack's wife Rita, worked right alongside of their husbands doing whatever had to be done. Feeding the stock, cooking, haying, wrapping meat just as the Crum brothers' wives had done.

The government regulations were getting so restrictive that it was hard for the Crum Meat Company to stay in business. In 1971 Hiram, Jack and Norman could see that the government would soon make it impossible for them to stay in business. At that time they decided to sell out.

The slaughter house was sold and only custom butchering was done in the once active commercial slaughtering house. Before long a fire late one night closed down the historic business site. A neighbor Al Bruce bought the original Merton Crum 160 acre homestead with the three homes on it and what was left of the slaughter house. It was saved enough that the Bruce family can still use it to do their own private butchering.

The meat market in town was rented out for a time then sold. Hiram went on to sell real estate after many years in the meat business.

Norman moved to Hat Creek to manage the Wilcox Ranch. Jack did custom butchering for a time then started a pottery business.

Businesses come and they go and some live on forever in the minds of many that knew it like it was. Such as the Crum Meat Company. Orville, Hiram, Allan, Donald and Norman are still here to tell the stories of how it was and are proud to share their experiences with those of us who care.

Glorianne Weigand
August 18, 1994

A True Cowboy and His Pioneer Lady

June 5, 1907 a happy bouncy baby boy was born just south of Adin, and at the age of 87 Alva Bennett is still bouncy and happy. Making all those that meet up with him happy to be around him.

Alva's grandfather George Whistman Bennett walked from Illinois and drove cattle all the way when he was sixteen years old. When he got to California he stayed at Emigrant Gap for a while. There he met up with the Wilson family. Making friends with this family was important to him as he would later take their daughter as his bride. After a time there, George traveled over the mountains to Portola and then on to Milford.

George and his young bride put their oxen to the yoke and traveled to Adin to make their home a mile south of Adin. There they started their farm and family. It was here that their son Arthur Bennett was born and was raised. The family milked cows and raised horses to farm their homestead with. Arthur later married Rita Nash and in the same house that Arthur was born in, their children Aristine, Alva, Emma, Alice, Noel, Neil, Elbert, Glen and Lucille were born.

Alva was raised in Big Valley and he and his sisters and brothers went to school at the Providence School house. Some of the pupils at the Providence School were Norma Studley, a small boy that Alva had to help on his horse named Haskell Parks, and Dorothy and Francis Fillingim.

Unknown to Alva at that time, but one day Dorothy Fillingim would become his wife.

Alva worked hard as a young boy. He could drive a six horse hitch and plow the fields before he was even big enough to harness them. His father raised cattle, horses, alfalfa and grain.

When it was time for Alva to go to high school he went to Susanville to seek his higher education. Even though his sister went with him they both were so homesick that they came back home to his parents. Alva went to work for a neighboring rancher, Vet and Dot Niles on their ranch at Butte Creek and worked there for about four years.

56

The years of feeding cows in heavy deep snow at the Niles Ranch were hard, but Alva speaks of them with fondness. He drove the team pulling the bob sled through the heavy snow to get the hay to the cattle in the winter. He drove the teams to put the hay up in the summer and rode many horses. One little black mare Alva was extra fond of he rode over to visit Dorothy Fillingim on. As he was riding her she dropped dead beneath him from sleeping sickness.

After Alva finished school he went to Susanville and worked in the box factory for four years. In 1930 he and Dorothy Fillingim were married and they moved to Willow Ranch where he ran a pool hall for a year then went to work in the mill. After the Willow Ranch Mill burned down Alva drove logging truck for a while. Not really caring for that he moved back to Susanville. In 1935 Dorothy's father Barney was beginning to retire and they asked Alva and Dorothy to come to Bieber to run the farm at the Bassett hot springs for Barnie and Bessie. July 8, 1936 a son Ronnie was born and was the delight of the family. Dorothy passed away soon after that and left Alva with a young son to raise. Alva stayed on and helped the Fillingims for several years then decided to make a new life for himself.

Alva heard that they were looking for someone to run the Doyle Ranch at Susanville. He had some cattle of his own and this seemed to be a good opportunity. He went to work for the Doyle brothers and worked for them for eighteen years. While at the Doyle Ranch Alva worked teams of horses to do the haying with. Alva always appreciated a good saddle horse and said he had some real good ones he rode through the years. Most of his horses he bought from Pierce McClelland.

At the time he left the Doyle Ranch he was running the ranch on shares, but still would like a place of his own. He and his wife Louise bought a place at milford in 1956 and they lived there for twenty two years. In 1978 Alva decided maybe he would slow down a little bit so he sold his place and moved to the Ross Ranch and took care of that place until Louise passed away.

You can't keep a good man down is the old saying and in the case of Alva Bennett he dug into his work and kept right on going.

In 1986 Alva married a long time friend Hilda Bass. Hilda's husband Warren had passed away some time before. Alva and Hilda were both 79 years old when they were married and combined the happy families.

Hilda had raised her two daughters Janice and Garneth after their father, Ches Long, passed away at an early age.

Hilda had worked at the box factory then went to the court house to work and had held the position of Lassen County auditor for many years. Hilda and Warren had bought the ranch that they lived on in 1950 and she worked in town while Warren worked the ranch. Building their dreams together.

Hilda & Alva Bennett with the Romagnola bulls.

Hilda was raised in Lassen County near Standish on a ranch, and her parents were Fred C. and Lena Farwell. Even though she was raised to be a farm wife, that didn't mean she was meant to be a teamster. She tried her best though and went out to help her husband mow hay with a team of horses. One horse was well broke and one was young and foolish and wanted to run. The young horse started to run but the old horse just walked in a circle letting the youngster run circles around him. Hilda got scared and jumped off of the mowing machine and broke her ankle severely, she lay in the field while the chattering mowing machine ran circles around her.

The ranch that Warren and Hilda bought was part of the Dieter Ranch. It had been inherited from the Dieters by the Hoffmans and they bought it from the Hoffmans.

When Hilda's husband Warren took sick they asked their daughter and her husband, Janice and Dale Flux, to come run the ranch for them. Janice and Dale had been leasing a ranch at Doyle. They were well known for their good Hereford cattle. Janice was born in Lassen County, but Dale had come there in 1947 to work for his uncle. In 1948 they were married and raised their family of four children, Judy, Ruth, Tom and Cheri.

Around 1984 Dale and Janice thought it would be a good time to try a crossbreeding program in their herd. A new type of cattle had been introduced from Italy known as Romagnola. Fairly new to the United States, only being introduced in 1973. The big grey docile bulls were impressive.

The Romagnolas were proven to be superior in many important qualities when compared to other breeds of cattle. The new breed of cattle is a massive, hardy, lively, yet docile breed highly regarded for its fast growth rate and excellent lean meat quality. Mature Romagnola bulls range from 2,500 to 3,000 pounds, while the cows average from 1,400 to 1,800 pounds. The heifers are usually bred at 15 months of age. Romagnola cows are well known for their ease of calving. The calves are sturdy, alert and usually up and nursing quickly after birth.

The Flux family bought their first Romagnola bull from Joe Covington and were on their way to a new enterprise. They were a little leery so they weighed each calf as it was born. The Romagnola, Hereford crossbred calves only weighed five pounds more at birth than the straight Hereford. But the proof came at the scales at sale time when the crossbred calves were weighed individually and the crossbreds weighed up to 100 pounds more than their straight Herefords.

Dale and Janice were so impressed that they went to Arizona and bought two full blood cows with heifer calves at their side. They were on their way to raising Romagnola bulls for their own herd and for show and for sale.

Dale & Janice Flux with their Romagnola cattle.

The pure bred Romagnola cows on the ranch now are up to twenty head and they have several bulls for sale. The calves weigh 80-95 pounds at birth and are a light tan color. By the time they are three months of age they turn grey in color, with black nose and eyes. The crossbreds with the Herefords are a light red with a white face.

Janice is the Romagnola lady of the family and as she said they are her babies. She and daughter Sherri and some of the grandchildren do the showing of the cattle. They show them at the Lassen County Fair, Shasta District Fair at Anderson, Houston, Texas, California State Fair and Cow Palace at San Francisco. The trophies of all styles line the walls and shelves of their home to show how well they have done as exhibitors at these events. Garth, a prize bull of the herd has been champion bull many times over. At the California State Fair a three year old female won reserve champion with her six month old calf.

Six bulls and one heifer will be sold at the Reno Romagnola sale March 26, 1994. There is quite a demand for these beefy animals as there are still not too many of them on the market.

While Janice is showing the cattle, Dale is running the ranch and the commercial herd which they run on the U.S. Forest Service. During the drought years the Forest Service cut the Flux range permit in half, but they are promised to have it reinstated this year. The commercial cows are sent to Anderson, California on pasture for the winter.

The Romagnola crossbred cattle do well on the range and utilize the forage extremely well. The Fluxes tried an embryo implant program, but the success rate of the cattle roaming the mountains did not prove to be worthwhile.

To keep their Forest Service permit the ranch has had to build fences and do quite a bit of improvement on the government owned land. Two years ago Alva and the grandchildren put in three-quarters of a mile of four barbed wire fence on the forest. The Forest Service had flagged it through trees, rocks and brush to let Alva know where they wanted him to put it. He has put in twenty-seven days of building fence when he was well passed eighty years old and supposed to have been retired.

Hilda's other daughter and son-in-law Bob and Garnie Pinneo live nearby and the families enjoy the closeness. Bob and Garnie have three children, Ronda, Ginger and Rob. On Hilda's side of the family there are seven grandchildren and sixteen great grandchildren.

Alva's son Ronnie Bennett and wife Bobbie live at Fort Jones, California where Ron is a logger and works draft horses. On this side of the family there are four grandchildren Rob, Dave, John and Lee Ann, and seven great grandchildren.

Alva is proud to be the last living charter member of the Lassen County Sheriffs Posse, of which he still goes to meetings and pays his dues. During the war they were pretty active with a lot of cattle rustlers. They would take turns and patrol the woods at night. Several times they have been called out to do important duties.

Alva and Hilda live an active life and are proud of their families and their ranch and love to go out and pet the gentle giant bulls of the Romagnola breed. They have both lived an adventuresome life and look forward to many years together. A true delight to visit and to hear of their escapades.

Alva is one of the true old cowboys and Hilda is a lady of the pioneer west. Love and laughter abound in their home.

Glorianne Weigand
March 8, 1994

Somewhere Between Nevada and the Ocean

Shawville, California, elevation 4270, population 3, Monroe, Bob and Billie. This is the sign you see as you approach the Shaw Ranch north of Lookout, California, at the end of Gougersneck. As Monroe puts it, they live somewhere between Nevada and the ocean. It's a good place to live as you can tell the four seasons. Early winter, mid winter, late winter and next winter.

What was once known as Craig, California in the early 1900's with its own post office and school is now a remote ranch in Modoc County. The road that meanders through the ranch was the first road between Oregon and California and where the Oregon Trail met the Applegate Trail, traces of the old trail are still visible in the upper corral of the ranch.

Monroe Shaw, at the age of 90, is still the straw boss of the Shaw Ranch and his son Bob is the ram rod. Bob's wife, Billie does as all ranch wives do, the cooking, cleaning, haul me here, help me there sort of jobs.

The Shaw family tree branches back to Monroe's dad Jasper when he was in Tennessee during the Civil War. Born in 1853, Jasper grew up in a hard and fearful time. Jasper and his brothers were out hoeing corn one day when a bunch of bushwhackers came by and wanted him to shoe their horse. Jasper was a blacksmith by trade, but did not like the looks of these outlaws. He refused to do the job for them. They said if he did not oblige them they would burn his blacksmith shop down. They proceeded to set the fire and Jasper was quick to accommodate the thieves. One horse had several sacks of money tied to the saddle that they had stolen. Even though Jasper did not ask for pay they paid him with the stolen money and they went on their way.

The Shaw homestead was at Cottontown, Tennessee, close to Nashville. They could hear the cannons being shot off and were near the fighting. This is when Jasper decided it was time to head to another part of the country. He had two brothers in Iowa so he went to visit them. There were too many cyclones and he really didn't like it there so in 1879 he packed his horse and headed to San Francisco. After a time he followed the coast north into Humboldt County. The winter of 1879 and 1880 was so severe and the

62

ranchers did not put up hay in that part of the country. When the cows started calving, they killed the calves to save the cows. This was very disturbing to the young Shaw, so he decided to look for another place to live.

Jasper had heard of the gold mining in Lassen County at Hayden Hill and thought that could be an interesting place to be. He boarded the stage coach with his saddle horse tied behind and rode into Hayden Hill. Jasper went to work at the Juniper Mine, the richest mine on the hill. One of the miners got hurt and one of the other miners was going to borrow Jasper's horse and ride for the doctor. No one but Jasper was ever able to ride that horse, so he had to ride to Adin for the doctor.

While working at the Juniper they had an old horse that was so smart that no one had to drive her. She pulled the whim in the mine to pull the loads up out of the shaft. All by herself she would pull the loads to the dump pile or to the pay dirt pile whichever the case may be. Then one day she just quit and balked and got lazy on them, so they had to have a boy drive her after that. While working at the mine Jasper fell 22 feet but landed in the soft dirt. He decided this could be a dangerous occupation also.

Jasper ventured over to Gougersneck and bought a homestead from Andy Eades. He went into debt so he rented it out to John Gould for six years and he went to Adin and worked in the store for Roseberry and Knight.

John Gould was a master barn builder. He would cut all the pieces and lay them out on the ground. When he was done with the cutting and hewing of the timbers all the neighbors would gather and in one day they would have a barn raising. He never used a nail in his barns. The timbers were all cut square by hand using a broad axe. The timbers were then raised up and tented, morrised and pinned to secure them together. Many of the barns that he put up may still be standing in the valley today.

Jasper would go back to the Craig post office to collect his mail and met up with the postmaster's daughter Eula Craig. A romance was begun and soon Jasper took Eula as his bride. They were married in Adin in 1901 and later came back to the homestead to take care of Eula's elderly folks.

The Craig post office was in the home of the Craig family and a room was built on the end of the house to accommodate the facility. The stage horses were kept at Craig as they would need a change from the previous postal stop of Lookout. The next post stop was at Dalton near Tulelake. When the winters were so hard the stage could not get through, the mail was carried on skis. When Jake Eades ran the mail he would ride wild horses. They would be pretty well broke when he got to the next mail stop. One time he got stranded in the snow and had to catch another wild horse to ride to the next stop.

Ed Craig was carrying the mail on skis and went snow blind. As he passed one of the homesteads the farmer's dog barked and saved his life. He would have kept on skiing and gone deep into the lava beds and probably would not have survived. It was quite some time before he regained his sight. Mike Welch, and John Robinson also carried the mail during the existence of the Craig, California post office from 1905 to 1915.

Jasper was 50 when he married Eula and she was 35. Monroe was their first born and he weighed 10 pounds at birth. The second child, Herman died before he was a year old and a third child, a daughter, Ilene died at birth. Eula had the measles when the baby was born and the baby got the measles. Monroe said he was the only tough one.

Jasper acquired the Craig homestead and traded Gene Ostrum ten head of cows and a jack mule for his 160 acre homestead. In 1883 Jasper bought another 160 acres from William Cantrall for $700.00. At this time Jasper was running 80 cows. Jasper raised quite a few horses and sold them to the McCloud Lumber Company. Some would be broke to work and some were not. Jasper also made his living by raising cabbage and potatoes along the river to sell to the stores, or trade. The Shaw family also milked cows and made butter to sell.

At hog butchering time all the neighbors gathered and helped each other do their butchering. Jasper let his hogs run on the river and they were two years old before they would butcher them. They took care of six or more hogs at a time. Every bit of the animal was used. They cleaned the intestines to make link sausages. The lard was rendered and the sausage was put down in a wooden barrel and the lard was poured over it and the meat would keep for a year. Hams and bacons were smoked, head cheese was made, the feet were pickled. As Monroe says, they used everything but the squeal.

Monroe had to start school at the age of four so they would have enough students to keep a teacher and the school. Most of the teachers boarded with the Shaw family. Craig was the school and it was the richest school district in the valley due to the Red River Lumber Company owning so much land and timber in the area. Monroe said he hated school then and never did like it, so after the eighth grade he went to Adin to high school for a few months and quit for good and went back to help his dad on the ranch. Later on he went to Healds Business College in Santa Cruz for a very short time.

Around 1916 the Shaw family would go to Santa Cruz to spend the winter. It was a three day trip in their Model T. Silas and Irene Myers would stay at the ranch to feed the cows. While there, Monroe was offered a job in a store but decided to come back to Modoc County.

The hills around the Shaw Ranch were a good hideout for many bootleggers. It was close enough to Klamath Falls, Oregon that they could haul their moonshine up there and get a good price. One of the bootleggers had such a heavy load on his wagon as he was leaving Crank Springs that he got stuck. He offered the young Shaw an unheard of price of $200.00 to pull him out. Monroe's team could not pull him and broke the chain, but they had to finally

Eula, Joseph and Monroe on their way to Santa Cruz.

throw a few barrels off of the wagon to lighten the load enough to get out. One of the moonshiners froze his feet so bad he had to cut his toes off with his pocketknife, using his own medicine to kill the pain.

The coldest winter that Monroe can recall it stayed 40 degrees below zero for a month. It froze Pit River clear to the bottom and the cows had to eat snow to survive. The snow was five feet deep and the cows were walking over the fences and he had to build fences on top of fences to hold them.

Monroe recalls many stories of the wild country that he grew up in. Shootings, hangings and fires were all a part of the rugged country.

Frank Hall, who was one of the five men hung for cattle rustling on the Lookout bridge, was a neighbor of the Shaws. Monroe said his father thought Frank was a good man, only he ran with the wrong crowd.

The day of his Grandpa Craig's funeral the Allen homestead was burned down because of a feud among some of the folks.

Old Ed Kennedy's horse was found with blood on its mane. They found Ed and he had been shot when he was on his way home from buying butter. The tub of butter was hung in the tree near where Ed was found and it hung there for a long time. There were inquiries but none of the mysteries were ever solved. This all happened in the vicinity of the Shaw Ranch.

Cattle drives in the remote northeastern part of California were always a way of life with most ranchers. It was no small task to get your cattle to market and took days or weeks to get to the nearest rail head. November 1921 a cattle drive was originated at the Weigand, Studley and Chace Ranches near Adin. 350 head of cattle was bought by Eddison Faulk from Kasper Weigand, Frank Studley, Ferd Chace and Author Criss and he wanted them driven to the Mitchell Ranch near Doris, California to pasture. The drive was ninety miles and it would take about a week if they could travel fifteen miles a day.

The five cowboys that started the cattle out were Lawrence Weigand, Herb Petty, Walter Kenyon, Author Criss and Rollie Rollison, a young cousin of Lawrence's from Missouri, but the first night when they got to Shaw's, Rollie got sick, so Monroe took his place and rode a horse that belonged to Ferd Chace.

The second day of the drive the cattle were driven from Shaw's ranch along the road about seventeen miles to the John Spaulding Ranch. A Mr. Beeler was staying in the two story ranch house there and he was a strange man and a spiritualist who believed in ghosts. He was afraid of the dark and wouldn't go outside after dark, and he would not walk through a gate. He

Monroe, Jasper & Eula Shaw.

would lay his hand on a post and jump over the fence. This was in the days of the bootleggers and good bootleg whiskey was referred to as jackass. Herb Petty asked Mr. Beeler, "You got any jackass?" The 70 year old man was a little hard of hearing and didn't quite understand. "No," he replied, "I took all my mares down to Mr. Mitchell's." The cowboy was sure the old man knew what he was talking about, but was just putting him off. Then Herb ask, "You got any ghosts around here?" Beeler replied, "Goats, when I had goats I had a little money."

Ferd Chace was camp tender for the trip and would follow along as best he could in his automobile and bring food and water for the buckaroos. Mr. Beeler was about out of provisions so he was glad for the cowboys to stop by and cook up a good meal.

Beeler never homesteaded his place, but just built a cabin on the Forest Service and they could never run him off. Mr. Beeler was killed when his team ran away then the Forest Service took his property back.

The third day on the trail got them to the Dalton place near Dry Lake. There was not many places to water the cattle, but here Monroe ran a horse-powered pump at the well to get water for the stock. The pump had two arms on it and revolved like a merry-go-round. One arm led the horse and the other was hooked behind him. The well went dry before all of the cattle could be watered. They started out about noon and headed toward the lava beds. They camped that night at Cauldwell Flat where there was only rocks and juniper. Ferd Chace met them there with food and water for men and horses.

While they were at Daltons, Tuck Courtright was staying there. Tuck said that Mr. Faulk that had purchased the cattle thought hay grew on bushes and water fell from the sky. Herb Petty was still in need of some moonshine and asked Tuck if he had any jackass. Tuck said he only had some Watkins liniment. But Herb refused the offer.

The next day's drive they were in the lava beds and they found enough water in Bear Paw Cave to give each horse a bucket of water, but again there was no water for the cattle.

Somewhere near Bear Paw, Sam Fleener had a place where he made moonshine and they happened on to him. Fleener knew Monroe's mother so he gave them a quart of moonshine. One bottle he had was 115 proof but he didn't offer that to the young cowhands. They hadn't had any food that day and the worst thing they could have done is to drink the whiskey. They rode on and made a dry camp that night. They had missed the trail and had gotten into the heavy lava beds and were lost. The camp tender Ferd Chace could not find them so they had nothing to eat at all that night.

Author Criss was the only one that had been in this country before when he had ridden for the JF Ranch. That night after dark, Monroe was riding watching the cattle when suddenly his horse stopped and refused to go on. Monroe dismounted to see why the horse stopped. There was a shear drop off at the edge of a rim rock. His horse had saved his life.

It was so cold that they would set whole juniper trees on fire to keep warm. Each night there was a heavy frost and the cattle would lick the frost from the rocks to get a little moisture. There was plenty of bunch grass and dry grass for the stock to eat, but no water.

There was one dog on the drive that belonged to Author. One night the dog got separated from his master and in his attempt to find him ran through the cattle and stampeded them right in the direction that Monroe and Walter had just bedded down for the night. The cowboys wasted no time in getting on their horses and headed to stop the cattle, but could not control them. The cattle stampeded until they hit some heavy lava before they slowed down.

The next day they got the cattle straightened out and headed in the right direction and went on to Willow Creek not far from the Mitchell Ranch. When the cattle smelled the water, they ran through a four barbed wire fence as if it were not there. The riders were unable to stop the thirsty herd. When the men and cattle arrived at Willow Creek the horses looked like gutted snow birds from the lack of food and water.

The morning after they reached the Mitchell Ranch, the cattle were corralled and the brands were called out. Ten head of Weigand's cattle were missing. They were lost on the third night out and had returned to the Weigand Ranch.

Monroe, Herb and Author rode home in the car with Ferd Chace. The horse Monroe rode was sold at the Mitchell Ranch. Lawrence Weigand and Walter Kenyon rode their horses home leading the other two horses. Somehow the two riderless horses strayed. One showed up at the Philip Miller Ranch in Stonecoal. Lawrence tracked the horse and picked him up and went over the hills to his home. Walter followed the road home. This drive just about cured the young cow hands of any lengthy cattle drive. There were times when they wondered if they, the cattle or horses would survive.

In the late twenties a young school teacher from Berkely, California came to the remote country to teach school. Her name was Rebekah Chance. Monroe and Rebekah started courting and on June 18, 1930 Monroe took a Chance for his bride. Their first child Bob was born in 1931 and Jane was born July 1933.

Rebekah and Monroe moved in with Jasper and Eula in the old home that had housed the Craig post office in one room. Jasper passed away in 1934 at the age of 81 and Eula died the following year.

Lightning hit the phone line quite a ways from the Shaw house in 1944 and it traveled down the line and burned the old home down. Many memories

Wedding picture of
Monroe & Rebekah Shaw,
1930.

and mementos of the past were destroyed. A house was purchased several miles away and moved in for the present ranch home.

Rebekah taught school for thirty years in Adin and Bieber. She had taught in the Modoc one room school near the ranch for six years. During the severe winters Rebekah would rent a cabin in Adin. In 1952 when Bob and Jane were both in college Monroe spent the most severe winter by himself feeding the cows.

One year Monroe went out to check on his cows. He came upon the largest herd of the largest buck deer he had ever seen. He went back to tell his cousin Price Craig and some of the other neighbors and they were going to have a big hunt. They stalked the bucks and when they spotted them over the rim rocks they started shooting like mad and sounded like an army. The firing ended and the bucks were gone and they never shot one of them.

One of the mistakes Monroe said he made was putting in a gas station for the Shell Oil Company. It was in the days when cars had to fill their tanks quite often, but he said the only time he did any business was during hunting season. He was glad to close down.

Monroe, Bob & Rebekah Shaw.

Bob went to Cal Poly after high school then returned to the ranch. Bob married Billie Lawson in 1969. Rebekah passed away in 1970 and Jane passed away in 1991.

Today the Shaw Ranch consists of 1260 acres and the Pit River runs through about two miles of the ranch. A rock quarry was started in 1966 by a highway building company and is still in operation and is rented by Modoc County. It is lava layered rock and it is run through a crusher and used for roads and asphalt.

Monroe broke many horses in his time and he used what he called a running W. He would tie both feet up and when the horses would run he would holler "whoa". If the horse did not stop he would jerk the rope and tip him over. "They learned whoa real quick," laughs Monroe. Some of the draft horses he would break to ride before he worked them, as he got older he would break them to work before he rode them. A team of draft horses is still used in the winter to feed the cattle.

Monroe, Bob and Billie live in a beautiful setting in a remote part of Modoc County and a welcome mat is always out for friends and neighbors to stop in for a visit at the S7 Ranch.

When asked if he ever wanted to do anything else, Monroe laughs, "If I had it to do over again I'd go to Hollywood."

Glorianne Weigand
December 15, 1993

Tales of an MC Cow Boss

It was just too cold. That is all Clevon Dixon can remember of going to school at Adel, Oregon. Riding your horse for miles to school when you are five years old is bad enough. But the winter of 1925 was very cold and little Clevon and his brother Cecil rode in the snow and wind to get to school. The school house was cold then you ate a cold lunch then rode the many cold miles home. So that is why Clevon quit school after the fifth grade. If you were going to ride a horse and be cold you may as well get paid for it. Clevon and Cecil started breaking colts when they were ten years old and now, Clevon, at the age of seventy-four is still breaking horses. Maybe not as many as he used to, but it hasn't been very long since he broke a horse. Something he loves and is very good at.

Breaking colts came easy to Clevon as he started that chore when he was ten years old. By the time he was fifteen he could buckaroo with the best of them. Clevon started to work on the MC Ranch at Adel, Oregon when he was seventeen years old and worked off and on for the MC for twenty-four years. During that time he held the prestigious job of cow boss for the famous MC. Other ranches he worked at were the Whitehorse Outfit in Oregon, Piute Meadows in Nevada and the Alvord, east of the Steens Mountains in Warner Valley. Clevon's and Cecil's dad Clarence Dixon started working at the MC before 1920, so it was natural for his sons to follow in his footsteps and go to work there in the line camps. Clarence raised cattle and horses himself, and also worked for the 7T Outfit and the JJ Ranch. The JJ had a ranch in Honey Lake near Susanville and they drove their cattle from near Adel to Honey Lake. A long hard drive and many miles.

Buckaroo pay at that time was $15.00 to $20.00 a month. You had to have your own bedroll, saddle and a rope. You slept on the ground in the summer under the stars and in a bunkhouse on the floor in the winter. Cowboys also had to have their own shoeing outfit and shoe their own horses. At one time the Indians braided rawhide ropes for the cowboys and they were furnished by the ranch. But this custom was taken advantage of and when cowboys left they took several ropes with them, or traded them for liquor.

Soon the rawhide ropes were no longer part of the gear given to the cowboys. Clevon braided a lot of rawhide ropes and liked to rope with them. During the long winters in the bunkhouse a lot of rope making was mixed with a lot of stories and tall tales.

The original MC Ranch at Adel, Oregon was started in 1870. William Kittredge bought the outfit in 1936. The Warner Valley Ranch was 21,000 irrigated acres. Another million acres of range land belonged to the Bureau of Land Management and leased range. There were 6,000 mother cows on the ranch at that time. Cows were only worth $6.00 to $8.00 a head so the cattle were almost thrown in with the deal when the MC was purchased.

Mr. and Mrs. Kittredge started their ranching venture at Summer Lake, Oregon where they milked cows and raised turkeys. Driving the turkeys to market was a long tedious job. To prevent them from having sore feet for the long drive they would walk the turkeys through warm tar then through fine gravel to coat the feet.

The Klamath Marsh Ranch consisted of 15,000 acres. The first 160 acres was bought from an Indian for a wagon load of groceries.

After buying the Warner Valley Ranch at Adel, the Kittredges drained the swamps and put in levees and dams and planted thousands of acres of grain and made a fortune when they sold their grain to the government during World War II for $50.00 A ton. The reclamation project of reclaiming the swamps was subsidized by the government. This helped with the huge expensive project.

During the depression when Clevon was thirteen and Cecil was fifteen they needed to make a little money. They took a pack horse and a pack mule and went out on the desert to gather wool from sheep that had been dead for a year or two. They worked hard and traveled far. They had all their camp gear on the pack animals. Their dad's good dog had followed them and they even had the dog on the pack horse with their huge sack of wool. They were afraid the dog would wander off and they would be in big trouble with their dad. They had been short of water and when they came to the lake the pack animals were very thirsty and dropped their heads to drink. One wandered a bit and got his rope hung up under the other animal's tail causing him to buck wildly. The bucking horse had the sack of wool and all the camp gear packed on him, which he deposited in the lake. The two young boys had lost all of their hard earned wool. Clevon and Cecil jumped in and retrieved all the camp gear and the soaked sack of aged wool and got it loaded back on to the horse. After several hard days work and many miles they reached their destination to sell their wool and made a whopping $7.50 for all their hard work.

Clevon started working for Mr. Kittredge at the MC in 1937. At that time Clevon knew the names of every horse on the ranch. Horses at the MC could be as many as 500 head at a time. Clevon loved this life, camping out in the desert with the cattle and horses. Cooking in a Dutch oven over an open campfire and sleeping in the open under the stars.

The buckaroos would start heading the cattle to the open desert late in March and never came home with them until November. The buckaroos really thought they were lucky when a chuckwagon and a cook was added to the desert cowboy camp. The buckaroos always had fresh meat to eat as they would butcher a heifer calf whenever they needed it. Their main diet was beans, biscuits, macaroni and canned fruit and coffee.

In the spring when it was time to start turning the cattle out it would take a month to get the chore accomplished. First they would turn out around 4200 dry cows the end of March so they would have their long drive of nearly forty miles over with by the time they started to calve in April.

In 1931 they drove the cattle to Greaser Lake, it was dry. They drove them on to Hart Lake and it was dry. They drove them on to Goose Lake and it was dry. They finally found water in spring holes to turn the cattle to.

In 1938 they turned the cattle out the 28th of March and it started to snow. It snowed two feet, and they had to gather the cattle and feed them for a month. When the snow melted and the floods came the cattle would be stranded on an island where they had gone to eat the bunched frozen hay. Clevon had to get a canoe and drive 60 to 70 head of cattle from an island and the water was so deep the cattle had to swim.

The yearlings were then driven to Summit Lake by the Adel cowboys and met half way by the Klamath Marsh cowboys. Mr. Kittridge also had a large ranch at the Klamath Marsh and this is where the yearlings spent the good grass months.

The next bunch of cattle that were turned to the grazing lands were the cows and calves. The MC ran around 18,000 head of cattle and it was a big chore to get them all to their proper summer pastures. Clevon claims that they had very little trouble calving the cattle out on the open desert. The cattle got plenty of exercise and the chances of scouring calves was unlikely due to open ground and a cleaner environment than a feedlot situation.

In the wintertime only cows with calves were fed hay. Dry cows were left to graze on the dry grass or the hay that had been bunched and left for their winter feed.

In 1942 Clevon decided he needed a lifelong partner that loved the ranch life as much as he did. Clevon had been born and raised in Adel, Oregon and just over the hill and across the California line there was a pretty young gal that was born in Lake City, California, Anola Hapgood. Clevon had just drawn his paycheck and he had $120.00 in his pocket so he and Anola boarded the bus at Lakeview, Oregon and went to Reno, Nevada to be married. Anola and her brother Hillard Hapgood were raised forty miles from Cedarville in Long Valley. Their Grandpa Jones had a freight line from Lake City to

Clevon & Anola, 1942.

Amedee near Susanville. They had a four horse team and he would haul flour from the two flour mills at Lake City and fruit or whatever needed to be hauled. He would bring back a load of sugar and coffee and other supplies.

After Clevon and Anola were married she followed him on his buckaroo jobs, helping out where she could. Driving the remuda horses while on the desert. The first four years they were married they lived at the IXL Ranch at Guano Valley. The MC leased it from the Sheldon Antelope Refuge and they fed 800 cows and calves there that winter. Anola drove the Jackson fork and Leon pitched the hay and fed nine ton of hay a day.

Clevon started eleven head of colts that winter. They ranged from four to twelve years of age. To catch a colt they always would four foot them with a rope or rope them around the neck to catch them so they could put a halter on them. Clevon never broke a horse to lead before he started to ride them. He said, "Why waste your time teaching them to lead if they can't be rode." He would tie up one foot, put his saddle on and a snaffle bit then ear them down, jerk the foot rope loose and get on. Anola would open the gate and off Clevon would go and Anola would just pray he would make it back. Clevon used both hands to ride and held on any way he could, because if he got bucked off he knew it was a long walk home. Clevon's theory is the quicker you can get out of a corral with a colt the better off you are. Clevon says, "If they spend all the time in a corral the colts get plumb soured and don't know what to do when they get outside."

Anola was a good rider, but could not rope and catch the horses, so if Clevon was not there to catch a horse for her she had to stay home. They were miles from nowhere and she always worried that if he got hurt, she had no way of getting help or going to find him. So Clevon knew he had to stick to those broncs like a feather on a bird and make a good ride and still be on top when he and the horse returned to the corrals.

After the cattle had all been turned out it was time to gather the horses and work them. Brand the young colts, cut out the older horses to be sold, sort the ones to be left with the stallions and castrate the young horse colts. It was always the job of the buckaroo boss to castrate the colts, because as Clevon tells it, he always got blamed if anything went wrong so he may as well be the one to do the job. Everyone has their own belief and custom for castrating a colt, but Clevon believes you should throw the testicles over the colt's head to make him run faster.

Shoeing some of the unbroke horses was a big job. Some you could shoe standing up, but some you had to throw down and tie their feet up. To accomplish this task you throw the horse and tie his two front feet together then tie his two hind feet together, then tie the front to the back. Then you put a pole between the feet and set about the job of shoeing your colt. If a bale of hay was handy they would use that to put between the feet.

Every cowboy had six to eight horses each and there would be about eight cowboys going out on the desert with the cattle in the summer time. They only used geldings as mares could cause a lot of problems while running a bunch of horses. The cowboys had their seasoned well broke horses and they had their desert horses that they rode at a run to cover a lot of country. The desert where they ran the cattle was seventy-five miles square and they had to move right along.

Keeping the cattle where there was feed and water kept them on the move and moving their camp constantly. It was easier when they had a chuckwagon and cook and the cowboys didn't have to worry about that chore.

After the chore of working up the horses was over it was time to start branding the calves. When the horses were branded the herd was driven to the nearest corrals and worked. But with the job of branding the cattle it was done out in the open, usually near a water hole where the cattle would gather.

Clevon kept his record book of how many calves they branded each day. One day in June while he was buckaroo boss they branded over 700 calves. The branding fire was built with cow chips. They would make a stack of the chips like a fire place and it would hold heat for a long time.

The MC at Adel, October 19, 1950.

Bill Davis on Spider, Clyde Reborse on Monarch, Ross Dollarhide on Salty, Howard McMullen on Dollar, Terry Cahill on Jimmy, Ray Vance on Little Beaver, Clevon Dixon on Floyd, and Dean Joplin on Colt.

The cowboys that did the roping on the desert would catch a calf anyway they could, and they would only use one rope on the calf, to save time and get as many done in a day as they had gathered. They would have six ropers and three ground crew. The MC brand was on the right rib, a swallow fork in the right ear and a waddle on the right side of the neck. The only vaccination that was given was blackleg. Many long hard days of branding were part of the job to get all the calves marked and branded.

One of the things that was a worry to the cattlemen was the wild plant, larkspur. If the cows eat it after a rain early in the spring it can be deadly. The first sign of larkspur poisoning is they start to limp, then they start quivering then they will go down. The only treatment at hand for the cowboys to give aid to the sick cow is to cut through the skin right under the tail and bleed the cow, then just go off and leave her alone. She will soon get up and follow the herd. In the fall the larkspur does not bother them.

One spring at turn out time the cowboys had to move 900 heifers ten miles. It had rained and the next morning 25 heifers lay dead from the larkspur.

A lot of cow bosses and a lot of cowboys came and went through the years on the MC. Even Clevon left a time or two to break colts elsewhere or try a different outfit. But Clevon was always welcome back at the MC and there was always a job waiting for him when he wanted to return. The first time he stayed for nine years and the last time he had worked there for eleven years. Most of that time as buckaroo boss, working cattle and living on the desert. Some of the cow bosses Clevon or his dad worked with were Leland Parker, Charlie McCleland, Virgil Miller, Garner Lundy, Sam Sweeney, Willard Duncan, Frank Pitcher, Ross Dollarhide, Hugh Cahill, and Dean Joplin. After that Clevon was cow boss. Gary Gooch and Donald Hill were some of the cow bosses after Clevon.

Cooks for the chuckwagon on the desert were hard to get and if you got a good one you were lucky. One that Clevon remembered was one that cured the cowboys of drinking coffee, and Clevon still does not drink coffee. The cook was a woman and spent most of her time reading a book. She would put wood on the fire and drag it across the coffee pot letting wood chips and bark drop in the coffee pot. The cowboys would have to pick these out of their cup as they tried to enjoy their morning cup of brew. The cook never took the old grounds out of the coffee pot, only added more each day. After she left the cowboys cleaned the coffee pot out and at the bottom of the pot the grounds had turned white. Another cook was not so bad, just sloppy. One day Clevon rode up in time to see the cook scooping the stew up off the ground where he had accidently dumped it. He was putting it back in the pot to serve to the buckaroos. Clevon said maybe the buckaroos could eat it, but he would not, so he fired that cook.

When Ross Dollarhide was cow boss he wanted Clevon and Duff Young to go to the rye grass and gather the cattle. The rest of the buckaroos were to come help them the next day. They rode the 40 or 50 miles to the camp to spend the night. All that Clevon could find was some hotcake flour, so for supper they made hotcakes. The next morning without even a bed to sleep in they had hotcakes again. Then they started to gather cows and gathered all day and still no one showed up to help them. That night they were lucky enough to find a can of string beans and that was supper. Still, no one showed up to help them to drive the cattle, so they started out by themselves and got to the buttes by sundown.

Dogs were not used on the desert to help drive the cattle. It was just too hard on them. The cowboys had eight horses to change mounts, but a dog had to cover all the ground that the fresh horses did and it was just too much for them.

Clevon wasn't much of a bridle man, but one of the good bridle horses he had was Taffy. No horse is fool proof, and when he roped a bronc out of the bunch on Taffy he turned the wrong way and the rope got hung up under Taffy's tail. Now no self-respecting horse likes to have a rope under their tail, so Taffy started bucking. Clevon did not expect the turn of events, but when Taffy made the first jump, Clevon landed on Taffy's neck in front of the saddle, the second jump he landed back in the saddle. The third jump he landed behind the saddle and the fourth jump Clevon was standing on the ground behind Taffy. That was one of his memorable rides.

In 1937 the MC culled 2500 old cows and they had to drive them 118 miles to market. The old cows would just wander around in the wrong direction and they could only drive them 18 miles a day. This cattle drive took them eleven days.

1941 Clevon came from the desert to wrangle horses for the hay crew. They ran twenty horse mowers and nine rakes. The work horses were wild as they were only brought in and used during haying season. Clevon spent most of his time retrieving mowing machines and rakes from where a runaway team had left them.

The pay for a man in the hay field was $2.00 a day. Some of the men went on strike and asked for $2.50 a day. Mr. Kittredge came to the field and told the men they would not get the raise, and anyone that wanted to leave could do so. About half of the men packed up and left. The other half were standing in the field. Mr. Kittredge told the ones that stayed that their wages would be raised to $2.50 a day. The happy men went about their work and were glad they had stayed.

The mosquitos and horse flies were so bad in the Warner Valley it was hard to work. The horses would just mill around and stomp all night. The men had to build smudge fires in their tents at night to be able to sleep.

In 1947 Anola worked for the MC for a few years as bookkeeper, did the laundry and housework and ran the commissary for the big sum of $4.00 a day. She did this for two and a half years then quit. While Clevon was cow boss Anola would go to Lake City and stay while he was out on the desert with the wagon.

Clevon's brother Cecil had many a horse wreck, but in 1939 one horse went over on the top of him and broke his shoulder and banged him up severely. The horse died the next day from the accident. Cecil never fully recovered from this accident and was crippled the rest of his life.

Clevon was riding a colt and as they opened the gate to let him out to the open spaces the horse hit a woven wire fence and bent Clevon's leg backward. He was left with a crooked leg for most of his life until he had a knee replacement.

Clevon did some rodeo riding when the entry fee was $5.00. In Cedarville he won third in bareback, third in bulls and second in wild horses. For all three events he won $26.50.

Riding night herd in the winter could be a harsh ordeal. One night while Clevon was on duty the thermometer dipped to 40 degrees below zero at Plush, Oregon. The cattle were so restless all night and just wandered in circles.

When Clevon came back from the Whitehorse Outfit to the MC they had seventeen colts for him to start. He worked for a couple years then was made cow boss for the next nine years. He held that prestigious job from 1957 to 1966.

The MC had a ranch boss, grain boss and the cow boss, so Clevon could put all of his attention to his job. Each entity had its own crew, boss and cook house.

Two of the things that Clevon did not like were mares and mules. Mares were trouble makers and he watched mare mules steal a colt from a horse and try to mother it only to starve it to death because she had no milk. A male mule would grab a horse colt in its teeth and just shake it to death. Clevon says a mule will try to kick your head off if he gets a chance.

After Mr. Kittredge died in 1958 things were not the same on the MC. Clevon stayed on as cow boss until 1966. He did not like the way things were run by the Kittredge heirs and the other new owners, so he decided to quit. He and Anola bought a little place in Lake City and Clevon did day work for the ranchers around there. He shod horses for $8.00 a head and rode colts

Clevon and orphan colt.

for $3.00 a day. When Clevon quit the MC in 1966 the monthly wages were $450.00. Quite a ways from the $20.00 he started with.

The famous MC Ranch has changed hands many times through the years and many famous cowboys have rode their horses there. One young cowboy, Ross Dollarhide Jr. became world champion steer wrestler in 1953. He then went into the movies and was a stunt man. A horse fell with him causing a lung to be punctured by broken ribs and he lost his life due to that accident.

Clevon was hired back by the buyers and sellers of the MC to count the cattle that were to be sold with the ranch. The number he counted at that time was 18,000.

With a quick wit and a memory that is amazing Clevon can tell stories of the good old buckaroo days for hours. With a twinkle in his eye and a delightful smile he is a pleasure to listen to. Cowboy poetry is another one of Clevon's talents. Anola has a lot to share in the history of the eastern Oregon desert. A true cowboy and his wife that tell it the way it was, living the buckaroo life on the famous MC Ranch.

Glorianne Weigand
July 13, 1994

Seward & Laura Kresge, wedding picture 1903.

Pioneers of an Untamed Land

When old man Gouger from the neck came to town everyone would take notice. He was a cranky sort, and called himself King Gouger. It has even been said that he got his name because he was so ornery that if he didn't like a person he would gouge the eyes out of their livestock. Today the long, narrow valley nine miles northeast of Lookout, California in Modoc County is still known as Gougersneck.

Many families and stories came about in Gougersneck. The Pit River runs through the neck and was a prime place to homestead. How people such as the Nathan Seward Kresge family who were descendants of Conrad and Anna Kresge from Switzerland ever found this small corner of the world is a mystery. Conrad and his brother Sebastian came to the United States in the early 1740's to make their mark in the world. Conrad followed the mining and farming field, while Sebastian went into merchandising. He started with small stores and markets and finally became the founder of the "K Mart" stores as we know them today.

July 4, 1875 John Kresge had come with his parents Conrad and Anna from the east by train. The buffalo were so thick through the plains they shot buffalo from the window of the train. Conrad and his family came in to Gold Hill, Nevada now known as Virginia City. Here he worked in the mines for three years then they heard of the homesteads in California so they headed to Gougersneck by mule train. They left the wagon train near the town of Adin and camped there that night on a knoll above town. The next day the family loaded up their wagon and went on to Gougersneck to their 160 acre homestead.

The family had very few belongings. They had one cow, a team of horses and a few chickens. The grass was so tall the children could barely find the milk cow that was out grazing. They would just have to wait and see where the grass was moving. There were no fences, but a few sheepherder camps were scattered through the valley. The family lived on deer and wild game. The valley was not too plentiful of deer so trips were made to the lava beds to hunt for their winter meat.

When all of the children were born the family consisted of John and his wife Mary and seven children. Emma (married Warren Green), Jervis (married Laura Fenner), Seward (married Laura Miller), Carrie (married Louis Kramer), Lenora(married Richard Nichols), George (married Maude Bennett), John (married May Berthume). George and John were twins.

Life was hard on the pioneer families. They had little to work with and had to build a shelter for their families as soon as they could. They planted crops of hay and grain. They would pray for rain to water their crops and when it came time to harvest them they would use a scythe and cradle. They would thrash the grain by putting it on the hard ground or on a canvas that they had used on their covered wagon. They then would ride or drive their horses over it until it shelled out. They would remove the heaviest part of the straw and then wait for a windy day to blow the chaff and finish their job.

Another problem was the giant Mormon crickets that plagued them. The children would go through the fields with tin pans beating them. The noise would drive the crickets from the crops.

For those ranchers that had cattle to go to market the nearest place was Marysville, California. The ranchers would group their cattle together and it would sometimes take a month to drive them to market.

In 1887 another family came to make their home in Gougersneck. All the good land had been homesteaded so the John Gould family took up a homestead and timber claim at Crank Springs. On their way to Big Valley and Gougersneck at the north end of this vast valley they had come to Anderson, California by train. They spent the night at the train station and the depot burned down that night and they lost all of their belongings. The Goulds were originally from England and worked their way to California from Michigan.

After the fire at the depot they bought a buggy and two horses. The two smaller children and the mother rode in the buggy while the two older children rode the second horse bareback and the father walked. Camping along the way they made their way to their new homeland. They came to Fall River Mills, then into the Whitehorse country, Egg Lake and Crank Springs. They homesteaded what they called Starvus Gulch.

John was a carpenter and he built a log cabin for his wife and four children Earl, Will, Agnes and Oliver. The cabin was built and still stands on the Monroe Shaw Ranch today. The neighbors helped John run down and catch a wild cow to use for the family milk cow. Fred and Alta were born after the family settled in Gougersneck.

In 1890 the Goulds moved to the Jasper Shaw place. The rent was half of the profit. Here they had a few more cattle and a few more horses. After living there for awhile they bought the Baker place which was 160 acres. The down payment was $50.00 and a total of $1400.00.

Another family that made their way to Gougersneck was Ira and Minnie Nichols. They came from Jackson County Oregon to Modoc in 1898. Minnie's family had come to California by wagon train that was being organized, but found it was cheaper to come by railroad to San Francisco. They soon went north to Salem, Oregon then into Idaho near Moscow. There they had to live in a stockade because of the hostile Indians. Later they also moved to Jackson County where Ira and Minnie were married. Ira contracted typhoid fever in 1896 and the doctor sent him to a dryer climate. The complete belongings of the family consisted of 15 head of cattle, a saddle pony, a covered wagon and one horse to pull the wagon. A team was needed to pull the wagon and the Nichols had a neighbor that also wanted to go to Modoc and he only had one horse so the families came together. After they arrived they went to work for Ira Cannon. Minnie milked cows and Ira worked on the thrashing machine. In March of 1900 they bought the Jenkins Ranch. The family had five children, Thurston, Bassie, Opal, Mapel, and Laurel.

The Kresge family was hit by hard times in the winter of 1879 and 1880 as well as the other ranchers of Gougersneck. The snow was so deep and they had no feed for their cattle. The men went on snow shoes to the mountains to cut mahogany branches and would bind them together and pull them like a sled back to the valley to feed their cattle. Day after day this was the ritual.

The Kresge family were good friends of the Indians even though the Modoc Indian War was in progress. Signal fires could be seen all around the valley. One old Indian would come to the Kresge home and he had a liking for sugar. He would say, "Me want sugar, me want sugar." Mrs. Kresge would put a teaspoon of sugar in his hand. He would lick and lick and say "um, good good." He would leave and in a few days come back and asked for more sugar. This went on for quite some time and Mrs. Kresge was getting tired of it. Sugar was expensive and hard to get. One day when the Indian came and said "Me want sugar," Mrs. Kresge said, "I'm all out of sugar, but I have some pretty red pepper you might like," the Indian held out his hand and Mrs. Kresge poured some cayenne pepper in his hand and he proceeded to lick his hand. He yelled, "Hot, hot" and ran for the horse trough. He never again asked for sugar, but was still friendly and came to visit.

In 1903 Seward Kresge married Laura Miller from Stone Coal Valley and they moved to Canby where they ran a trading post. There Laura gave birth to twin sons Owen and Orin. Orin died soon after birth. After two years there, they moved to Adin where Seward built a beautiful home for his family. In 1906 through 1911 Seward and Laura Kresge acquired 350 acres from several land holders, namely Goochman, Rice and Smith. All the land was in what is known as Round Valley.

Marcel on Seward's lap, Owen and Laura Kresge.

After moving to Adin two more children were born, Marcel and Leola. The families started to mingle, court the neighbor girls and weddings were soon taking place.

Oliver (Ollie) Gould married Bassie Nichols in 1914. They met in Gougersneck. After they were married they went to Lakeview for three years. They then came back to Gougersneck and moved on Ollie's folks' ranch. Their children Cedric, Edna and Bonnie were born and raised there. They went all eight years of grade school in a one room school then on to Adin to high school. At that time they would board the bus at 6 a.m. And get home at 6 p.m. as the bus would skirt the full portion of Modoc County in Big Valley.

One of the bus drivers was Owen Kresge, son of Seward Kresge. His mother was looking for help to cook for the hay crew and he asked Edna if she would like the job. Not only was there a job but Owen had a younger brother Marcel that made the job much more enjoyable.

Winters at that time were severe and lots of snow. Cars went into the garage the first of October and stayed there until the first of May. The ranchers would have to use sled and horses or breaking cart to get to town in the winter.

In the winter of the deep snow of 1936 and 1937 there was no hay in the Sacramento Valley and there was lots of loose hay in the barns in Gougersneck. Stationary balers were sent up to bale the hay so it could be sent to the valley by truck. As Gougersneck was nine miles from Lookout and the roads were snowed in they used caterpillars and sleds to transport the baled hay back to Lookout to the trucks. This caused the roads to be well packed down with a sled trail.

Marcel Kresge had been courting Edna Gould and he had a new 1936 Buick that he was pretty proud of. He heard the cat tracks had the road packed down to Gougersneck so he decided to go for a visit. Marcel stayed later than he planned, so the family convinced him he should spend the night. During the night the weather warmed up after weeks of below zero weather and the road was slushy. Not able to travel on it with his Buick he had to stay for five days. By then his future father-in-law Ollie Gould had to tow him all the way to town with his team of horses.

In 1937 Marcel and Edna were married. They moved to Round Valley and built a cabin on the Conklin place where Owen lived. They lived there for two years. At that time they ran a trap line to make enough money for a winter grub stake. They trapped coyotes, bobcats and muskrats. They would get 8 to 10 muskrats a day and sold the hide for 50 cents a piece. It took all day to ride their trap lines as they were the entire circumference of Round Valley.

After two years they leased the John Kresge place, and ran it for three years. They were not allowed to sell any female cattle, no matter how old they were. Only steers were to be sold. At that time they sold steers for 8 cents a pound.

Marcel's dad had decided he wanted to retire and wanted to sell so Marcel and Edna bought him out.

Owen was on the Conklin portion of the ranch and had gone to college and business school for a time and he was working for the A.S.C.S. office in Alturas.

When Marcel and Edna left the John Kresge Ranch they got the increase which was 200 cows. To make a fair division of the cattle the neighbors were asked to come in and sort the cattle for them. This gave them a good start on their own ranch.

Before the trucks were available to haul cattle and before the railroad had come to Big Valley, cattle had to be driven to Madeline to be put on the railroad. This was at least a two day drive and neighbors would put their herds together and sometimes have as many as 300 head to drive. The first day they would drive them twenty miles to the Stone Ranch in Ash Valley and spend the night. The next day on to Madeline. One night while they were sleeping the cattle broke through the fence and headed back toward Round Valley and were nearly home by the time the cowboys caught up to them. At that time a good steer would sell for 4 to 6 cents a pound and a fat cow 2 to 3 cents a pound. One time Seward was offered 1 cent a pound for a cow and would not

Marcel Kresge and his winter trapping.

sell her so he butchered her and loaded the meat in his wagon and peddled the meat to his neighbors.

While Owen was working at the A.S.C.S in Alturas he met the home demonstration agent Betty Walters and they were married in 1946. Owen soon decided that office work was not for him and he went back to Round Valley and went into farming and ranching full time. Betty and Owen had two children, Paul who never returned to the valley after his college graduation and Jane who did return home to her parents' ranch after college. Jane married Jim Copp and they bought Owen and Betty out when they retired. They also own Copps Irrigation in Adin. They have three children Julie, Jana and Perry. Owen passed away in 1992.

Marcel and Edna bought the home ranch from Seward in 1943 which was 1280 acres and in 1952 bought out Smith and Holbrook. In 1965 they bought the McClure and Daisy Harper Meadow from Tom Barrows. Making their total ranch of 3000 acres.

Marcel and Edna spent the next 32 years on the Kresge home ranch. The depression made for hard years, but they survived it with hard work and fortitude. Marcel and Edna had two sons, Glenn and Gary. The whole family was very active in 4-H. Edna was their beef leader as well as any other projects the boys decided to take. She has been a leader for 17 years and Marcel was community leader for 15 years.

After the boys got out of college the family went into a corporation. Glenn married Darlene Edgerton in 1958, they had three children Jerry, Martha and Brad.

Gary decided he wanted out of the corporation so Glenn and Darlene bought the ranch from Marcel and Edna as they were ready to retire. In 1975 Marcel and Edna remodeled the home on the Smith Ranch and moved there. Glenn and his family moved to the home ranch.

Glenn ran the ranch and was an order buyer for local cattle for the Harris Feedlot. In 1977 Glenn drowned in a ranching accident while crossing cattle at the Pit River near Bieber.

Hunting and fishing was a way of life with the Kresge family and Marcel and Edna enjoyed many good times with these sports.

After retirement from the ranch Marcel and Edna decided a fun thing to do would be to work on a fire lookout for the Forest Service. They put in their application and there was a vacancy sooner than they expected.

The first year they were sent to Sugar Hill off of Goose Lake on the Warner Mountain District at 7200 feet and 30 mile an hour wind in a tower 45 feet from the ground. This was to be their new home for the fire season. Two green horns were now two fire watchers. It rained for six weeks and they were sitting in the clouds and couldn't see a fire if it was a mile away. They were very lonesome, Marcel went to fire training with the crew every day, but Edna was just staring at the clouds. For fourteen years they worked on the lookout towers at Sugar Hill, Round Mountain and Blue Lake and really took a liking to it. By the first of May each year they were anxious for their summer vacation on the mountain.

Marcel's health started to fail so they ended their career with the Forest Service and retired full time. They enjoyed hunting, fishing and their gardening.

Marcel, who was lovingly called "Binko" by his grandchildren, passed away in 1987. On his mother's side of the family he was a fifth generation born Modocer and Edna on her father's side is a fifth generation born Modocer.

Brad and Martha have gone on to other occupations.

Left to carry on the Kresge tradition of cattlemen and ranchers are cousins and great grandchildren of Seward Kresge, Jane Copp and Jerry Kresge.

Jerry went to Billings, Montana to auctioneer school after he finished high school. He was on the home ranch for a while then in 1980 he married Lorene Wilson and they have two children Amy and Glenn.

Jerry is an order buyer for local cattle as was his father Glenn and is carrying on the tradition of ranching and cattle production as did his forefathers when they first came to Gougersneck in 1880.

Glorianne Weigand
September 15, 1993

The Bognuda Bunch From Little Valley

Clover and Lil, everyone has heard of the famous bronc riding Lil and her sister Clover. Life for these two was never boring and the tales they could tell would keep your attention for hours on end.

From the Alps of Switzerland to the mountains of Lassen County, known as Little Valley traveled Ned and Josie Bognuda. Around 1906 when Ned first came to the United States he was not married, but soon met Josie who was also from Switzerland, not far from where Ned was raised. They soon were married and lived in Clover Valley in Plumas County.

Their first daughter Cloverine was born there, and in 1912 a second daughter Lil was born. Ned was disappointed as he wanted a son more than anything. Through her life Lil proved to be more than a son to Ned, as she could do anything a son could do and probably better. Clover was the one to help their mother Josie with the house chores.

After eleven years in Clover Valley, Ned was tired of the hard winters and the grasshoppers and looked for a better place. He found a ranch in Little Valley in Lassen County that was 640 acres of meadow and a log home and some outbuildings on it. Ned drove his 150 head of cows and Josie drove the 1912 Michigan car. They traveled from Clover Valley to Willows to Ned's brothers Siro's place and after a stay there they traveled on to Little Valley. Clover had to stay at Willows as the climate at Little Valley did not agree with her.

After the family settled into the log home in Little Valley Josie would travel back and forth spending a lot of time in Willows with Clover.

Lil loved the ranch life as a young girl and loved it her whole life. She would ride her little horse eight miles to the Dixie Valley Ranch to play with the Indian children as that was her only playmates.

The year of the first annual McArthur Rodeo Ned took Lil to see it. This is where Lil saw her first lady bronc rider Annie Engle. Lil decided then and there she would become a lady bronc rider also.

91

When Ned bought the Little Valley Ranch it was pretty run down and needed a lot of repairs. Dick McGrue came to work for Ned and stayed on for twenty years.

When it was time for Lil to start the first grade she went to Willows and stayed with Uncle Siro and she and Clover went to school.

Cattle prices were looking good and Ned decided to built a new house. He had to haul the lumber sixty-five miles from Pondosa by team and wagon.

Lil was not happy at Willows and wanted to come back home to be with her dad on the ranch. She felt she learned more by working there even at her young age than she was learning at school.

Lil had many hard knocks at a young age. One day curious Lil was watching the men work while sitting on the top log of a log corral. A corralled wild horse jumped the fence and knocked Lil off. She was unconscious for quite some time and spent two weeks in bed.

Lil was lonesome with Clover gone. An Indian, Lyman Lamarr worked for Ned. Lyman had quite a few children and Lil was happy to have them to play with.

Siro decided to come up and go into ranching with Ned. They called themselves the Bognuda Brothers and used the JB brand to brand their cattle. Siro did not like the Little Valley, so moved back to Willows.

The Bognuda's were milking a lot of cows and raising a bunch of hogs to feed the surplus milk to. One day Clover and Lil were playing and opened the spigot on a tank of soured milk, letting the hogs have their fill. Before it was all over seventy hogs laid dead in the lot. Both girls got a whipping from Ned that they never forgot.

Ned bought 150 Hereford cows from Roderick McArthur and he started in the beef business. To take the cattle to market they had to drive them past Hayden Hill to Madeline to meet the railroad. Lil started on these drives at a very young age.

Lil started to the first grade for the second time at the Pitville School and lived with the Vestal family. She also lived with the Ingrahm family. Lil still did not like school.

Steer prices were six cents a pound and times were hard. The Dixie Valley Ranch was the hub of the cattle country, with hundreds of riders and thousands of cattle being gathered and separated there. While turning the cattle out the Forest Service would try to count the cows on to the range. This was never a very successful job.

Ned started milking more cows and making cheese to sell. There were tales of moonshine being made in the hills around Little Valley. Times were hard and you had to make a living any way you could.

Lil and Clover entertained themselves with their made up games. Their favorites were wild cowboy, wild Indian, bank robbers and wild white kids.

Ned had a school built at Dixie Valley and Lil started the first grade for the third time. Clover was doing well in school and loved her studies. But Lil would rather be on a horse. A lot of Indian children went to school at the Dixie Valley School and Lil and Clover learned a lot from them. Their learned their customs, beliefs and lifestyle. Some of them were their best friends. And a lot of them stayed friends throughout the years. Lil was proud that she knew all the Indian cuss words.

Ned was a good friend to all the Indians and they called him "Bug". Arthur Barnes worked for Bug for many years, an honest and hard working Indian.

Clover liked to drive the Model T Ford to school, but Lil would rather ride colts. It was one way of getting them broke.

A cousin, Ray, came to live with them when he was in the second grade. His mother was Josie's sister and she had died. Ray and Lil soon became real buddies. At first he was a pain, but soon learned to do chores, milk cows and ride colts.

The children had no toys, so they used pine cones and empty bottles. The cones were cows and the bottles were their horses. Ray and Clover used string for harness to tie the bottles to a box for the wagon. Clover was the beef buyer, paying for the pine cone cows with broken glass for money.

At an early age Lil started to rodeo by racing her little black pony. She was so excited when she was paid $5.00 when she won a race at the McArthur Rodeo.

Haying was always a big headache to Ned, but a chore that had to be done. Clover and Lil both started driving teams at an early age to drive the buck rakes. Ned always drove the lead mowing machine as he would have at least one runaway a day and no one wanted to be in front of him. Ned didn't have the patience with a horse that Lil did. He had no fear or respect for them, which is why when he slapped a slow moving colt on the rump one day he kicked up with both feet and kicked Ned's front teeth out.

Dick McGrue broke most of Ned's horses. The horses liked him and he was a good hand. Ned raised a lot of good saddle horses and registered Percheron draft horses. Gelding saddle horses were rode and mares were only used for breeding. After Dick rode a horse a time or two he turned it over to Lil to finish breaking. Even at an early age Lil had an uncanny understanding of horses. Clover and Lil were both bucked off more times than they could count, but climbed right back in the saddle. Lil could remember several good long hard rides, like driving cattle to Pondosa, a 130 mile round trip to load the cattle onto a train.

Clover graduated from the Dixie Valley School and a big dance was held. Everyone joined into the festivities. Ned and Josie were afraid that the only way to get Lil and Ray out of school was to burn the school down. When Lil finally did graduate she had to go to Bieber for her graduation ceremonies. To her disgrace her mother made her wear a dress for the occasion. One of the few times in Lil's life she ever wore one of those frilly things.

Clover went to Reno to a business college. She came home after graduation and Ned bought her a new Model T Ford for a present. The family said Clover was a walking encyclopedia.

Lil would rather stay home and run a trap line trapping coyotes and bobcats. Running wild mustangs at the sand hills was an adventure for the young cowgirl. Some of the cowboys that helped Lil corral the wild horses were Leonard Johnson, Floyd Walker, Harold Vestal, Fritz Bunselmeir, Bill Thompson, Sie Elliott and Dick McGrue. What an exciting time that was.

Ned was beginning to loan horses out for rodeo bucking stock. Lil was getting into the bronc riding more often as she grew older.

Some of the cowboys Lil rode with were Roy Swain, Bill Whitney, Bill Vineyard, Charley Snell, I.C. McCall, George Reterath and Bill Dennio.

The McArthur Fair and Rodeo was a highlight in Lil's life and she only missed three of them in her entire lifetime. The great old cowboys and cowgirls that influenced Lil so much were ones she rode with there. George Farmer, Bill Robbins, Dorothy Morrel, Annie Engle, Perry Ivory, Coyote George, Arizona Kid and Roderick McArthur.

Clover loved wild pets and always had fawns, chipmunks, coons, a red fox and even a porcupine. Living among the wild animals and caring for them was a pleasure to Clover.

Buck hunting was a way of life in Little Valley and big bucks were plentiful. Hunting became a business as so many hunters were stopping in and bringing all their friends. Ned started charging for their room and board. This was an enterprise that soon was very successful.

Clover and Lil were traveling all over in Clover's new Model T. They were hitting all the rodeos from Red Bluff, Marysville, Reno, and Lakeview. They started the circuit in the spring and went until fall. On the way to Alturas to a rodeo, Lil was driving Clover's car. A noise started in the front end, and even though Lil was driving plenty fast, she started driving faster. Finally Clover told her to stop and see what the noise was. As she slowed to a stop the front wheel fell off of the car.

One of the rodeos in Reno Lil rode exhibition on a chute fighting son-of-a-gun. She had to mount him in the middle of the arena. He bucked into the fence and stuck his feet in the hood of a new car with Lil still aboard.

In the spring of 1929 Little Valley came to life. The Western Pacific Railroad started putting their shiny rails, tunnels and bridges through Little Valley. They moved in tents, surveyors, contractors, trucks and dozens of men.

Lil & Clover.

Lucky Bug, as people called Ned, was right in the middle of all the Western Pacific hundreds of employees. Ned had contracted for everything from horses to equipment. Ned built a log bar, a dance floor and a rodeo arena. Ned sold rights of ways, cleared rights of ways, sold cedar posts, rented horses, boarded hundreds of people.

The W. Puckett Co., the Fredrickson and Watson Co., Baker and Taylor Co. were all there to build the railroad to meet the Great Northern Railroad at Nubieber. The rails were being laid just a mile from the ranch, so Ned reaped the benefits of the railroad while it was being built.

Life was lively and the Little Valley Rodeo was put on film along with the building of the railroad and showed at the Nubieber theater. Pictures of Lil were taken and used on rodeo posters all around the country. In the Little Valley Rodeo Lil rode broncs and Clover carried the flag in the grand entry. Montana Red helped put on the rodeo.

Lil always managed to get the rankest of the broncs. She was well seasoned as every evening after a day of haying they would have a little rodeo of roping and bronc riding.

On November 10, 1931 the golden spike was driven at Nubieber connecting the Western Pacific Railroad and the Great Northern Railroad. The construction of the railroad was over and hundreds of men moved out. The fences, corrals, water tanks still had to be built. The construction crew boarded at the Bognuda Ranch and Josie cooked for all of them.

The drought hit the ranchers hard. Hay was gone and cattle were turned to the range the end of January. Some starved, some made it. Again Lucky Bug was fortunate to have the railroad so close and he had hay shipped in from Tulelake.

It was wonderful to be able to ship the cattle from their back door instead of driving them for miles and miles. Some of the ranchers using the railroad besides Bognuda were Nelson, Hollenbeak, McArthur, Byrnes, Eldridge, C.W. Clarke Co. of Dixie and more.

Another venture was soon to fall into Lucky Bug's lap. Some timber men from Oregon came to inspect a stand of timber at Dry Valley. There was four feet of snow on the ground, but Ned took them to the timber site. With their approval a mill was soon to be built at Little Valley. A cook shack was moved close to the ranch and Josie and Clover cooked for the mill hands and timber fallers along with the Bognuda Ranch hands. Nearly forty people were fed at every meal. The log bar was moved up from the railroad tracks and a big sign was painted to put on the front that declared it the "Bognuda Club".

Little Valley was jumping once more, rodeos, dances and parties to keep the loggers entertained. In five short weeks all the glory was over for the Plum and Anderson Sawmill when lightning struck and burned the mill down. They never rebuilt.

Clover and Lil were hitting the rodeos hard. They rode at Willows, Peardale, Ukiah, Willitts, Lakeview, and McArthur. Clover decided it was time she did something so she took up a 640 acre homestead near her parents ranch. She proved up on it and was legal owner in due time.

Again Lil and Clover hit the rodeo circuit with their friend Roy Swain. Lil said he was one of the best cowboys she ever saw. While in Pendleton Lil rode relay against some of the best cowgirl riders, Della Schriver, Dorothy Hunt and Isabell Beldon.

Another crew to stay at the Bognuda Ranch was the Forest Service porcupine crew. They sent twenty young men with their 22 rifles to kill the porcupines that were damaging the timber. They killed 800 porcupine in and around Little Valley.

The Forest Service then sent the bug crew to cut down and burn all of the pine beetle damaged trees. The next crew that were sent to do a job was from the B.L.M. They were sent in to corral or shoot all the wild horses. The horses were shot and the landscape was dotted with the bleached out horse bones. The mustangs were all killed and a legend was ended.

Things were quiet at Little Valley and a little boring when in January 1936 the Welch Brothers from Dorris came to see about building another sawmill. A cook house, bunk houses and homes for the families were built. Little Valley was fast becoming a town. It was known as "out where the pavement ends, and the west begins". Ned built a ladies bar and it was named the Empty Holster. The loggers bar was too rough for a lady to enter.

The war came along and a lot of the loggers went to the service. The Welch brothers built a box factory and most of the employees were women. Lil worked in the box factory and Clover was the bookkeeper. People from every state were represented in the saw mill or the box factory.

A young cowboy from Virginia was working at Dixie Valley breaking colts. His name was George Corder and within the year Clover had met him and wedding bells rang.

Lil had a boy friend, Hack Lambert. In 1941 Hack was drafted into the army and was gone for five years. Hack had been working for the Clarke Company at Dixie Valley at the time.

Soon the Welch brothers sold their mill to some new men and they renamed it the Indian Head Lumber Company.

In 1936 Lil and Clover loaded up their horses and went to San Francisco to ride in the Golden Gate Parade. Some of those representing Lassen County were Pierce McClelland, Tom Johnston, John and Dorothy Capezzoli, Hank Stone, Wilma Spraker and Lil and Clover. Roping anyone or anything in sight was a big joke to the Lassen County bunch. It was a wonder they weren't thrown in jail.

George Corder started promoting rodeos around the country. Lil and George team roped together and Clover was the time keeper. George was a good roper and they all had an enjoyable time.

In July 1942 the C.W. Clarke Co. Sold the Dixie Valley Ranch to T.E. Connolly from San Francisco. Dixie Valley was settled in 1878 by the Reavis brothers and Clarke bought it in 1892. Bill and Hazel Spalding were the new managers of the Dixie Valley Ranch and were there for twelve years.

In 1943 George Corder went to New Mexico and purchased the first quarter horse stallion to hit that part of Lassen County. It was a seven-month-old colt named Teddy. George bought some quarter horse mares and soon was raising some of the best quarter horses in the country. His delight was to set in the evenings watching his horses graze in the pasture.

In 1944 Clover and George had a baby boy and named him George Ned Corder. Lil always called him Bucky, she said it fit him better.

Hack Lambert was still in the service and was sent overseas. Letters were few and far between. The war ended and Hack sailed home. He was discharged December 15, 1945. Hack went back to work at Dixie Valley and Lil helped him ride and gather the cattle. October 5, 1946 Hack and Lil were married in Reno. Hack and Lil moved to Dixie and lived in a one room cabin for a year then Hack quit and went to work at the mill. Hack had all the bucking, kicking biting colts he wanted for a while. And thought he would try something easier.

In 1948 Ned and Josie took a trip back to the old country of Switzerland to visit relatives. Hack and Lil ran the ranch and the bar for Ned the four months that they were gone. George and Clover bought a small ranch at Cottonwood and moved for the winter.

Hack went back to work at Dixie for a time. He and Lil did a lot of traveling from rodeo to rodeo. The Indian Head Lumber Mill burned to the ground in 1954 and things were at a standstill at Little Valley once more. Families moved out and the mill whistle that had blown regular for eighteen years was silent. The whole camp was auctioned off and was to become a dude ranch. This never materialized but another sawmill was built.

In 1955, Tom Connolly came to Hack and Lil's house and asked Hack if he would run the Dixie Valley Ranch for him. The job wasn't easy, but one that Hack and Lil handled proudly and were excellent at. They had good cowboys and some not so good. Good cooks and some not so good. They raised excellent horses and cattle.

Josie & Ned on a trip to Switzerland.

In back: George Sr., George Jr., Lil.
In front: Clover, Travis, Toby, Tarron.

In 1971, Tom Connolly tried to buy the Little Valley Ranch. The price was too high for 1617 acres. That was all that was left of Ned Bognuda's fine cow outfit.

In 1972 Lil was grand marshall of the Inter-Mountain Fair parade. She rode her proud buckskin gelding, Dutch Seven. Hack and Lil had spent many cold miserable winters in Dixie. They had good times and bad times. They enjoyed their job and Tom Connolly was a wonderful man to work for. But all good things must come to an end. In 1973 Hack wrote to Tom and gave him notice that he would be leaving Dixie Valley. The Lamberts were ready to move south to Red Bluff where it was warmer.

The rest of the Little Valley Ranch sold to a family in Ohio. Corder's rented it back for a few years, and George still enjoyed his horses.

The stories that were told around the old wood stove at the Bognuda Club were endless. Hunting stories, horse chasing, bronc riding and logging. If only the walls could talk.

Ned, Josie, George, Hack and Lil have all gone to the happy hunting ground in the sky. Clover and her son George, his wife Kathy, and their sons, Travis, Toby and Tarron are left to carry on the legend of the Bognuda Bunch from Little Valley.

Glorianne Weigand
May 15, 1994

Cowboy Reflections

A cowboy, a friend, a neighbor. These are all words to describe John Poytress. Cowboying has been John's life long love right along with his wife of fifty-seven years, Marjorie.

John is proud to call Adin, California his home. Born in Fresno County in 1912, he grew up on a little farm milking cows when he was big enough to sit on the milking stool. He then developed a new skill of picking up apricots for five cents for a fifty pound box. As he grew into teenage years he drove a derrick team to stack hay for fifty cents a day. He was really coming up in the world. Times were tough in those years and a young man would do most anything to make a dollar.

When he was fourteen he was hired on to drive cattle to the high country. Finally his cowboy dreams were coming true. Those drives took four days and they made three different drives during the summer.

On one of the drives the boss told John and his friend to watch the cattle. So like he tells the story, "We were like good dogs and watched the herd." Soon it turned dark and they realized everyone had left them. Not sure of their directions and not sure where camp was they remembered an old cowboy once told them to let their horses have their head and they would take them home. That is what they did, but by the time they got back to camp everyone was asleep and not at all worried about the two young cowboys. Supper was long over and with nothing to eat they crawled into their bedrolls. Only a few hours later the boss dumped them out of their bedrolls and told them to go catch a horse.

By 1931 a friend had returned from Big Valley in northeastern California with stories of the big cow country and you could cowboy all day, every day. Thinking they were seasoned cowboys they drove 530 miles in their old Model A Ford to fulfill their cowboy dream. With $35.00 between them they headed north. Gas was five cents a gallon in Fresno and in Adin it was an unheard of price of fifteen cents a gallon. Camping out along the way and eating at a donut shop now and then they made their way to Adin.

As they passed a ranch, John said this is where I am going to work. They stopped in and as haying was to start the next day, John got a job on the Lawrence Weigand Ranch and his friend went to work on the next ranch. Cowboying every day didn't seem to fit into the plan as cows were on summer range and hay had to be put up for winter feed. John drifted in and out of the Weigand Ranch for seven years. He would go back to Fresno now and then because that little pesky neighbor girl had grown up and he had taken quite a shine to her.

In 1936 John brought Marjorie up to Big Valley and they went to Reno to get married. That summer Marjorie helped cook for the hay crew at the Weigand Ranch and John helped put up the hay.

Returning to Fresno after that they rented a place, cows and all. In 1942 they ran a pack station and packed into the high country.

At that time, he received a letter from Mr. Frank Studley of the 101 Ranch in Adin and he wanted to know if John wanted to rent his ranch. A chance he couldn't pass up, John, Marjorie and their young son Jack moved back to Big Valley. A few years later their second son, Tom was born. Some of John's nephews were also raised by John and Marjorie.

Riding the range south of Adin and driving cattle from Big Valley to Honey Lake west of Susanville are some of John's fondest memories. Andy Knudson, Earl Clark, Floyd Walker and Mike Wayman were some of the seasoned cowboys that John rode with. Their first night on the long drive would be spent at the Avala place near Willow Creek, then the next night was spent at Grass Hopper. There they would meet up with Tommy Johnson and the McClellans from Susanville and then drive their cattle on to Honey Lake together. This was quite a treat as the Johnson and McClellan crew had a camp cook.

A long ride for several days not long before that really made a cook appreciated. After riding in the rain all day with Andy Knudson and Floyd Walker, they found and old sheep camp where they built a fire to spend the night. They were on their way to Dixie Valley and the ride was taking them longer than they planned. It was dark by the time they got the fire built. John was the young ramrod so they found some old bottles and sent him to the spring to get some water for coffee. They found an old rusty can and boiled the water and made coffee. Sleeping in the rain under sweaty horse blankets, they spent a pretty miserable night. The next morning they sent John after more coffee water. As it was daylight they could see all the mosquito larva swimming in it. But they decided as it hadn't killed them the night before they would make coffee again. They found some flour a sheepherder had left in an old can and made hardtack biscuits in a rusty old pan. John was not too thrilled with the dirty old stick they stirred the biscuits with. When they got

Stan Weigand and John Poytress.

John & Marjorie on John's 80th birthday, March 1990.

to Dixie Valley they never knew food could taste so good, as they hadn't had much to eat for three days.

After twelve years of the 101 Ranch, John moved to Canby where he rented a place from Ed Albaugh for three years. Then he took care of Mr. Quigley's cattle for three years. At that time he went to work for Roger Bacon at the Blacks Canyon Ranch for sixteen years. When Mr. Bacon sold the ranch, he sold John along with it to Oakley Porter. John finished the summer and helped gather the cattle off the range and decided it was time to retire. John and Marjorie built a home near Adin and moved back home to Big Valley.

Later when Porter sold the Blacks Canyon Ranch to Peg Brown, John went back and worked for her off and on for several years. He still helps out with the riding and working cattle.

After moving back to Adin he also worked for Nile Pearce irrigating and tending cattle.

Still today at the age of 81, all you have to do is say "Hey John, I need a hand," and he's there to help. He loves to ride with you, rope calves all day at a branding or shove cattle up the chute for their vaccinations. A better hand to castrate calves can't be found.

John loves the cowboy life, a good horse, a strong rope and a good story.

This is what keeps John Poytress young at heart with a hearty laugh and a line of stories that will entertain you all day long.

Glorianne Weigand
May 15, 1993

Thad Bath & Earl
McCoy, 1915.

The Stones And McCoy Pioneers

There is a valley in northeastern California in Lassen County. A beautiful valley that steals the hearts of all who have lived there. The lush meadows and the clear cool creek known as Ash Creek gives the valley its name of Ash Valley. The abundant wildlife and the trout in the stream were the livelihood of the many Indians that lived there in the late 1800's. Many families called these high mountain meadows their home when they took up their 160 acre homesteads in the 1870's and 1880's. Some of the homesteaders were LaPoint, Ballile, Sturdervant, Ben Bath, Chisholm, Williams, Grays, Molls, Templetons, Finnigan, Hawthorne, Holbrook, P.M. Walker, Fulstone and John Fulstone Bath, Spooner, Sisroe, Loveland, Slater and Dent.

The grandfather of Bertha Stone McCoy, John Fulstone Bath came to the valley in 1881.

As a young man Grandfather John Fulstone Bath came from Salt Lake City, Utah to Carson City, Nevada, with his parents. Their best ox had died and they could not travel on at that time. A man had come over Donner Pass and told them not to try to go on over the pass. Mr. Bath decided to stay and cut hay for the teams of the wagon trains going on to the California gold fields. He did quite well at that business and decided to grow gardens to sell the produce to the wagon trains as well. John sent to England for his nephew Ben Bath who was a wheel wright in that country. Later Ben Bath and Uncle Joe Fulstone had moved on to Ash Valley.

March 1878 John Fulstone Bath took Mary Ann Petrie as his bride in Carson City, Nevada. In 1881 John Bath visited Ash Valley and was impressed with the rye grass so tall that you could hardly see the horse's backs. He returned to Carson City, Nevada to bring his family to the new home he had found. July 3, 1881, John and Mary Bath and their two year old daughter Carrie and six week old daughter Alice arrived at Ash Valley after a long dusty trip with team and wagon. Carrie had tired of the trip and her mother kept her entertained by having her look at the pretty birds on the colorful tea tin in the wagon ahead of them. All her life she could still see the birds on the tea tin. They entered the valley from the south and Ben Bath came to meet them on a white pacer horse. They left the wagons and took the horses on to the Fulstone place to spend their first night.

John had bought a ranch and they moved into the two story house.

In 1897 a son was born to John and Mary Bath. He was named John Thaddeus Bath. He was sixteen years younger than his sister Alice.

The post office at Ash Valley was known as Ashton and Carrie Bath was the post mistress. There was a small building that served as the post office next to their home and the mail was delivered by horse drawn stage twice a week from Madeline.

February 23, 1898 a gala wedding took place in Ash Valley when Carrie Bath married Henry Norton Stone from Butte Creek near Adin. The wedding party was quite an event with a huge feast at midnight and the guests all dancing or playing games all night until the break of day when they could drive their teams and buggies home. The newspaper article told of all the guests and all the wonderful household items they received as gifts. Also they received 1,000 pounds of potatoes and a dozen laying hens.

Henry's father and mother, Norton and Mary Stone had crossed the plains in a covered wagon in 1854 with his uncle Willard Stone who was the captain of the wagon train. April 6, 1854 the group of 37 wagons left Illinois. Most of the travelers were young, only eighteen to twenty-five years in age. Quite a few were newly married couples. As they started traveling their hearts were gay and they sang to the stars. "Oh Susanna, don't you cry for me, I'm bound for California. The gold dust for to see."

This was not Willard's and Norton's first trip as they had been to California in 1851, but returned to Illinois to take sisters as their brides. The wagon train was known as the New Lebanon Company.

It was still spring time and the rain came in torrents and heavy snow. The cattle they were driving were hard to contain. They had to ferry across rivers. They could not buy feed for the stock and had to stop for them to take time to graze. At places they found corn for 12 cents a bushel and hay for $2.00 a ton. Fresh eggs were five cents a dozen. The farmers had good crops, but no way to market them and were at the mercy of the wagon trains coming through to buy their wares.

Traveling was hard and slow, mountains and rivers slowed them down. There were no settlers for miles and miles. They came to Council Bluffs on May 11 where the great Indian treaties were signed.

Many were sick and the train had to hold up for them to get better before they started across the five hundred miles of plains that would put them at Fort Laramie. Hundreds of people and thousands of cattle were camped along the Missouri River.

The women wanted to homestead there as they were already tired of the bumpy dusty wagon trains. They were afraid they would be scalped by

Indians. The young men had paid $50.00 a piece to join the train and they had promised to stand guard, drive teams and drive cattle, so they were committed to go on. It was rainy and gloomy as they crossed the river into Nebraska.

Captain Willard Stone was too sick to travel and the torrential rains had made the creeks too high and swift to cross. There were many Sioux and Pawnee Indians in the area terrifying the women. At night the Indians would steal their horses. One night they had taken seven horses and one mule. They followed the Indians hoping to retrieve their horses as they needed them to pull their wagons, but had no luck. It took extra time to cut timbers to make bridges to cross the swollen creeks.

They had started to cross the plains. Miles and miles of grass and buffalo. Nothing but buffalo chips to make their fires to cook their food with. They were making good time on the plains and some days would cover twenty miles. They passed many graves on the trail where people had died of cholera.

Finally they reached the Black Hills and Fort Laramie. They had traveled 500 miles. When they reached Fort Laramie they hoped there would be news from home awaiting them. But there was not a letter or note. Had everyone already forgotten the pioneers looking for a new land. The women were sad and cried.

On July 13 they reached the dividing ridge between the Atlantic and the Pacific with an elevation of 7,400 feet. This is where the waters of the melting snow and rain started to run the other way toward the Pacific Ocean. The traveling was easier as they were heading down hill.

They came to the Green River and had to ferry across for an unheard amount of $4.00 a wagon. The Mormons of Salt Lake City owned the ferry and had changed the signs that said there was a rocky ford a few miles down river.

The wagon train arrived to the point where the road forked. The Oregon Trail went to the northwest and the Snake River. Fort Boise went south along the Snake River. The train took the western route along the Oregon Trail.

The oxen and cows had such sore feet they had to be treated by drawing a small rope in between their claws to clean out the sand and gravel then the men would pour hot grease in the foot. The oxen had to be shod.

The mountains were steep and treacherous and they had to hold the wagons with ropes to keep them from tipping. They chained the wagon wheels together to keep them from rolling. Twelve miles a day was top speed.

Willard Stone bought an Indian pony from the Flat Head Indians to drive the cattle. John and Sol Gage had the mountain fever and Mary Stone was very sick. Grass was scarce for the stock and they were very restless and thin. August 2, 1861 they passed Raft River. The Indians were bold and would steal their horses. They now had fire arms instead of arrows and were not afraid to use them. Even though they were not good shots.

Sol Gage and Sid Terwilliger decided to drop from the train. They had started with 200 cattle and all but 125 had died and those were thin and sick.

September 5 they started crossing the desert. They had made hay for the stock and tied it in bundles. They traveled day and night to cross this barren land. Hundreds of dead cattle lay along the trail. The smell so bad they could hardly stand it. Tempers flared and brothers blaming brothers as their teams dropped in their tracks. They would put a few belongings on their backs and walk on cursing their oxen that lay dead on the trail with their yokes on.

They finally reached the Sierra Nevada mountains. The train ahead of them had all been murdered by the Indians and their wagons burned. Willard Stone had hired a friendly Indian and his squaw to travel with them to keep the Indians under control. The Modoc Indian War had been severe and they wanted no part of that.

The first of October they were near Shasta River and started for the Stone Ranch in Shasta Valley where their parents were. This would be the end of their journey. The trip had been 180 days of travel and 33 days of rest. On October 4, 1854 the weary travelers reached the golden land of California. Some stayed and mined, some scattered and some were so homesick they soon joined a wagon train headed east and went back home.

The above is a portion of the daily account of the wagon train written by Andrew Soule a member of the New Lebanon wagon train party.

Norton Stone who became the grandfather of the Stone children in Ash Valley was born in 1825 and died in 1891. After settling in California Norton Stone had built seventeen bridges across the Sacramento River. The high waters came in the winter and washed them out. He rebuilt the bridges and roads only to be washed out again. He had lost all of his money building the bridges and decided to try something else.

In 1870 he and his wife Mary moved to Big Valley on Butte Creek near Adin where he built up a beautiful homestead.

The son of Norton Stone, Henry Norton Stone took Carrie Bath as his bride. They moved to Butte Creek where their children Florence, Bertha, Ruby and Lloyd were born. In 1908, when Lloyd was only two years old and Carrie was pregnant with a child, Henry had fallen from a scaffold while working on the Providence Church. He had been in ill health due to gall stones for some time and this added to his problems. Some doctors traveling through Adin were known to be surgeons and operated on Henry. They found him to be full of adhesions and gave him only a few months to live.

Carrie was devastated and not knowing what to do with a family to raise. John Bath went to Butte Creek and moved his daughter and grandchildren back to Ash Valley to live with her parents. Her husband died at the age of

Carrie Bath Stone holding Lloyd, Bertha, Florence,
and Henry Stone holding Ruby.

34 leaving her with four small children. Their fifth child Henry was born a few months after the death of their father in 1908.

A large family to take care of called for a large home and John Bath had a 19 room house built. Thad was still a young boy at home and close to the age of his sister Carrie's children. The home was built from lumber hauled from Johnson Sawmill near Butte Creek and hauled in by freight wagons. They had the only house with running water, a bath tub and carbide lamps. The house was finished enough by Christmas that Thad could be the first to sleep in the house. There were eight bedrooms, a huge dining room, living room, parlor and kitchen and other rooms.

The Stone children loved their Grandpa Bath. He was a kind and gentle man. When he went to town he always brought candy home for the children. When they saw him coming down the lane they would all run to open the gate and receive their candy.

In the Ash Valley School in 1909 there were children from the following families. Stone, Bath, Slater, Whittenger, Massotti, Anderson, Highland, Loveland, Fulsone and three Indian children, the Carmony and Crooks.

In 1913 John F. Bath met an untimely death leaving a home full of women and children. Thad was only sixteen and not old enough to carry on the responsibilities left to him. Different members and friends of the family came to help out.

Carrie had to make a living for her family. She milked cows and made butter to be sent to the mining town of Hayden Hill. The freight teams took ore from Hayden Hill to Madeline to the railroad and had a barn near the Bath Ranch in Ash Valley to keep a fresh team of horses. There was a box on the outside of the barn where Carrie would leave her butter to be taken to Hayden Hill. She would wrap the two pound rolls of butter in a paper and a white cloth to send to the miners.

Ben Bath, John Fulstone Bath and little Hank Stone.

Grandmother Mary Bath was to deliver the butter one evening and she took Florence, Bertha, and Lloyd with her for the evening ride in her one horse cart. While driving along, some men were lying in the sage brush and jumped up and scared the horse. The horse bolted and ran. Mary had to do some pretty fancy driving to keep the cart from tipping over. Bertha still remembers the fright from the wild ride.

There were Indians in the valley that came and helped on the Bath Ranch. One was Old Sally that came and helped turn the wash machine on wash day. She lived in a very nice wig wam not far from the ranch. One day an automobile went by her place and she came to the Bath Ranch so excited. She called Carrie "Kelly." She said, "What ya callum Kelly, what ya call um. Hurry up go, getty up horse." She could not understand how anything could go without a horse in front of it. Sally always talked about the big "boom". That is what she called the Modoc Indian War at the Lava Beds.

Another Indian that helped out was Old Nancy that always wore a basket on her head. She lived in a sweat house made of rocks and hides.

All the work on the Bath Ranch was done with horses and many Indians helped with the haying. Grandpa Bath thought women should not be in the field, but were to stay in the house to do the cooking.

All the children went to the Ash Valley School. When they were ready for high school they would have to go to Adin and board with someone. Bertha was the first to go to high school as it had just opened. Florence went to Los Angeles on the train from Madeline and went to Bible college. Hank went to Davis to school. Then went to work in Susanville on a ranch. Lloyd went to Healds Business College for a time.

Groceries were ordered wholesale and brought in to Madeline on the train and brought to the big house in Ash Valley by freight wagon. They would go to Adin and buy a ton of flour from the flour mill there. In the winter you never went to town. The snow was too deep and it was too far. Bertha remembers one year when her mother only went to town one time.

One year there was an enormous amount of grain grown in the valley when they had an exceptional wet year. Neighbors to the Bath Ranch the DeForests bought a stationary threshing machine and everyone hauled their bundles of grain to the thrasher to be harvested.

When Bertha was eleven years old a boy of fifteen came to Ash Valley to look for work. He had been raised in the Fall River Valley and had been working in the Florens Store. He did not like being inside so when a hide buyer was heading to Ash Valley, young Earl McCoy caught a ride and came looking for a job. He went to work on the Bath Ranch and came back each summer for seven years before he and Bertha were married Sept. 20, 1921. Earl's family had moved around a lot and had moved to San Jose. Bertha and Earl moved to Fall River where Earl had bought a Packard truck and was in the business of hauling anything that needed to be hauled. They moved to Maxwell where he hauled rice and grape stakes. From there they went to Medford, Oregon where they bought a four acre berry farm. Later they traded it for 160 acres at Malin, Oregon. They were there when their daughters Berlva and Glenda were born.

Earl cowboyed for the Pitchfork Outfit at Tulelake owned by the Dalton family. He had a love of horses and sat straight in the saddle even though he walked with a limp. He said his limp was from too many falls from too many horses. Earl was a farmer and rancher and a friend to all. Earl loved to visit with anyone and he never knew a stranger.

When Earl was 77 years old he signed a contract with the Modoc National Forest to capture the wild horses that ran on the Devils Garden. Not many were interested in helping in this wild horse chase, so his daughter Glenda rode with him. First they had to build log corrals to capture the horses if they ever caught up to them. After the corrals were finished they started their daily routines of searching for the wild mustangs. After several hours ride beating the rocks they would spot the wild fleeting horses. By this time Earl and Glenda's saddle horses had tired with them being mounted and not used to the rocky terrain. They would take off on a dead run in hot pursuit of the mustangs. The mustangs were uncanny and knew every inch of the trails and juniper thickets. They were elusive and would give them the slip every time. Again the next day they would try the same routine and at the end of the day they came up with an empty corral as like the day before. Finally Earl decided the only way to capture the wild creatures would be with an airplane and he and Glenda's days of chasing the wild ones came to a halt.

John and Mary Bath's other daughter and her husband, Pit and Alice Walker decided to move back to the ranch and help out. They only stayed for a short time. Earl and Bertha also came for a time to help. Grandma Bath had help from Earl and Pit until 1924 when Thad ran the ranch. Thad and his family moved to a neighboring ranch in 1936. Thad continued running the home ranch with the help of Lloyd and hired help.

At that time steers sold for seven cents a pound and cows for five cents. Cattle were driven to Madeline to the railroad to be sent to market. In the earlier years when cattle had to be driven so far they were sold by the head, not by the pound.

Florence came home from Oakland where she had been teaching children's Bible classes. She had been away from home for twenty-five years. She stayed on to help as her mother was getting older and Lloyd needed her help. Lloyd nor Florence ever married. There were twenty to thirty men to cook for during haying season as at that time they were still using lots of horses to hay with. Breakfast was at six a.m. At 11:30 the huge dinner bell was rang or a flag was raised so the men knew it was time for them to bring

Lloyd Stone.

their teams to the barn to feed and water them while the crew was fed. At night time the men sat around and sharpened their mowing machine sickles while they swapped stories. Young girls were hired as cooks helper.

All has changed with the passing of Thad, Carrie, Lloyd, Alice, Earl, Florence and Hank. The Bath Ranch was split and the Stones sold their half of the ranch.

At 92 Bertha Stone McCoy is still happy to share her stories of her life and time in Ash Valley.

Glorianne Weigand
June 16, 1994

The Thompson Ranch

The IT brand on the right hip of Hereford cows at the south end of Big Valley means the Thompson Ranch is still thriving after 123 years on the same range. The Thompson brand was number 8671 registered in California by George Thompson in the 1870's.

The third and fourth generations, Bill Thompson and his son Bill Jr., are still very much in the cattle business and intend to stay that way. Although Bill is 87 years old he still puts in a long day on his horse driving cattle to and from the range. The unique thing about the Thompson Ranch, is that they border their Forest Service and B.L.M. range allotments so when they get the go ahead from those agencies in the spring time it is an easy task to take their cattle to their summer grazing grounds.

The beginning of the Thompson Ranch is attributed to Bill's grandfather George Thompson who came from Ireland in the late 1860's to New York. There he married his wife May. George was a school teacher and surveyor. He found his way to Fall River Valley like so many pioneers in search of their dreams. After two years they decided to move to Big Valley. There they took up a homestead along the Pit River and built their house on top of a big knoll. George surveyed and built the original road to the gold mining town of Hayden Hill.

George and his wife had three children. Jim, and his two sisters Hattie and Lucy. George died when Jim was only thirteen years old. Jim had to run the ranch for his mother. They could not find anyone that could drive the teams of oxen that they used on the ranch. They were building the many miles of split rail fences they needed to surround their ranch. Jim was quite a hand with the animals even at his young age. He was the official teamster of the oxen as they hauled the rails from the nearby forest.

Hattie never married and moved to Susanville where she was a clerk in Emerson's Department Store. Lucy was a teacher and married Tom Wilson who became sheriff of Lassen County.

When Jim became the rancher he had worked so long and hard for, he took Nellie Packwood as his bride. In the years to come Jim bought out several

Milt, Bill & Rex Thompson, 1929.

neighboring ranches to expand his own ranch to the present 4040 acres. Some of the homesteaders he bought out were Blask, Jones and McWilliams. The remains of the McWilliams' two story log home is still visible on the Thompson Ranch. This was the home of twelve children.

Jim and Nellie had five children, Rex, Faye, Milt, May and Bill. All but Bill left the ranch and went their separate ways.

Jim ran one hundred Belgium horses and used them for draft horses to hay and farm with on the ranch. He also raised them to sell for chicken feed. At that time they brought $7.00 a head for a thousand pound horse. They used catch colts for their saddle horses. They also raised one hundred head of sheep and two hundred head of cows. In 1937 they sold fed steers for three cents a pound and cows for two cents a pound.

In the 1930's, Nellie Thompson advertised in the Susanville paper needing a ranch cook. Louella Derrick had come to California from Missouri to visit her brother in Loyatton. After reading the ad, Louella came to Bieber to the Thompson ranch and hired on as a cook. She and Bill were both thirty-one years old and a courtship soon was on Bill's mind. Louella went back to Susanville and worked in the box factory for a while until Bill asked her to marry him. She then was the permanent ranch cook.

Bill & Louella Thompson, wedding picture 1930.

The three Thompson brothers with their dad; Bill, Milt, Rex and Jim Thompson.

Bill recalls a long miserable horseback ride in 1938 when he drove six head of their yearling heifers home from Little Valley (where they had strayed to) back to Big Valley. It was just over the hill, but was a nine hour ride horseback. The thermometer read 25 degrees below zero. He froze his feet severely. They swelled to twice their normal size and were extremely painful. He was lucky not to have lost them.

Bill went to Healds Business College when he was a young man for a while. When he returned to the ranch from that venture he never left again for any length of time.

Bill and Louella have a son, Bill Jr., who runs the ranch now with his father's assistance. Bill still runs the swather on their alfalfa and grass hay

Bill Thompson.

fields. What once took dozens of men and horses months to hay is now done by two men. The nine wheel lines keep them busy moving them.

The Thompsons run nearly 500 head of cattle and put up all the hay for the cattle. The winter is spent feeding all the hay that they put up in the summer. Calving, branding, doctoring and riding the range for the cattle is an enormous job in itself.

In 1984 on the 4th of July, Bill's horse fell in a badger hole and rolled over on him. After laying in the field for three hours, he was found and taken to the hospital where he spent six days. Both bones in his ankle were broken and he had three pins in his leg as a painful reminder. An enlarged ankle keeps him from wearing cowboy boots, and it is hard for him to mount his horse.

Bill, Louella, their son Bill Jr., his wife Starla and son Sam and daughter Heather still keep the tradition of the Thompson Ranch and their heritage very much alive.

(Bill passed away after the writing of this story and he is sadly missed by his family and friends.)

Glorianne Weigand
June 1993

Free as a Breeze, and Wild as a Sagebrush

As I drove up the dirt road to the Shepherd ranch I thought of all the children that think Charlie Shepherd is Santa Claus because of his white flowing beard. I felt I was going back in time as I drove through the juniper and pine trees toward the homestead. A few deer grazed with the cows in a meadow along the road and as I approached the home of this intriguing family, I was met by the family dog and mother hens searching for food for their tiny feathered chicks.

As you travel out of the tiny town of Lookout a few miles along the railroad track, you will approach the Shepherd homestead. Several homes and trailer homes are part of the family dwellings.

I soon came to reality as I saw 93-year-old Charlie Shepherd out hoeing in his garden in the warm morning sun. What most of us consider a garden would hardly be a taste for the Shepherd family. The rows of his well groomed garden are four hundred feet long. He had ten rows of corn, two rows of zucchini squash of which they can over one hundred quarts for the winter. Three rows of beans, rutabagas, carrots, onions, and beets not to mention a huge rhubarb patch. Charlie used to raise potatoes and sell them to help with the income of the family. The garden is the stable lifeline of the family as well as all of their own meat they raise. Sometimes they have as much as five hundred quarts of fruit and vegetables preserved in their root cellar.

Charlie pointed out to me that he had no bugs in his garden and as I surveyed the situation I could not see one bug hole in any of the leaves. He explained the reason and as we checked the garden there were about ten small bantam hens with their babies picking every bug in their path.

"People think they need bug sprays and pesticides," explained Charlie, "when all they really need is a few chickens in their garden". Charlie is a true believer in the Almanac when it comes to planting his garden or caring for his animals.

As we visited we were joined by fourteen-year-old Lester, one of Charlie's grandsons that live on the farm with the rest of the family. Lester reached down to pull a weed that is one of my most dreaded pests in my

120

garden. I thought how nice, he is helping his grandpa, but to my surprise Lester started eating the weed that is known as pursley and is a very healthy herb. It is used by the family as a green at their dinner table, and has a radish taste to it. They mix it with scrambled eggs and meat and it makes quite a tasty dish.

Charlie is well known in the valley for his herbal medicine and natural healing. He has been studying this skill for over fifty years. As with the pursley most of us have no idea what they are good for. I was soon made aware of many of the plants around the huge garden. Mint was one of the most used and I was familiar with mint tea for a stomach ache, but never used it for a cold. The comfrey is made into a tea and used for cuts, wounds and infections. Wild carrot is the cure for intestinal problems and flu, honey is used for burns as well as aloe vera. Horehound plant is good for colds and making candy. Charlie said he could cure a cold or sore throat overnight by rubbing the throat with mentholatum, then rub on pure turpentine and drink one half glass of dark wine with one half teaspoon of ginger, juice of two lemons and honey to taste. Wild carrot will also cure ulcers. For summer complaint or flu, chop six inches of the root of button weed and boil for thirty minutes and drink the tea. Another good cure for a cold that Charlie had heard of is to kill a skunk and use the oil from their sack and rub it on the chest.

Lookout, California in Modoc County is the home town of this witty gentleman and his extraordinary family. Charlie says some people call him a character, but he is almost a legend in his time. Charlie says he was a rolling stone most of his younger life. He would walk fifty miles in a day to get to the county seat of Alturas. He describes himself as "free as a breeze and wild as a sagebrush."

Life has been an adventure for Charlie. Born in Harrisburg, Pennsylvania, December 1, 1900. His mother was upstairs giving birth to this infant son while his father was downstairs trying to keep the home from floating away in a flood. There were ten boys and two girls and Charlie was the oldest.

When Charlie was four years old the family left Pennsylvania and moved to Indiana. His father was a bridge builder and a farmer. He was also and Indian fighter in the U.S. Infantry in Nebraska. When Charlie was seven years old he can remember running a cross cut saw with his father. His father was a giant of a man at six foot four inches and 265 pounds. Charlie did not get the size of his father, but had phenomenal strength. Charlie started driving a team of horses when he was nine years old.

Charlie left home when he was twelve years old to go out on his own and never saw his mother or father again. He started working on farms in Indiana. By the time he was fourteen he was working on the section gang for the New York Central railroad. When he was eighteen on Nov. 7, 1918 he was called into the draft. But the armistice was signed on the 11th of November, so they

Charlie Shepherd.

didn't want him. The next spring they called him again and he went into the "lighter than air force," the balloon observation corp in World War I. He was a first class balloon mechanic. He was sent to Missouri then to California. He then served twenty-six months in Hawaii territory in 1919-1921.

While in the Air Force he was the champion heavy weight boxer. He beat the Navy champion in four rounds and the Marine champion in three rounds. He nearly killed a man boxing him, so he quit the sport.

When Charlie got out of the service, he went to work in Los Angeles as a stone cutter. He didn't like town and was worried about all of his co-workers having lung and eye problems because of the stone dust. Charlie started working with the Anderson Power Company and PG&E and came to Pit 4 in Caton Valley. "After the unions took over, I quit, I didn't want anything to do with them."

Charlie loved to work teams of horses and drove eight teams at a time with one jerk line. He worked with the teams pulling large harvesters, freight wagons and logging.

Charlie had fallen in love with the rugged country of the Big Valley so he decided to finally settle down and make a home. In 1934 he had been working on a ranch for Homer Roberts and fell for the daughter of one of the men that worked there. Charlie and Clara Selby were married, he was thirty-four and she was eighteen.

The next year Charlie bought his present home site from Louis Kramer. He bought thirty-one acres that the railroad had cut off from the Kramer Ranch for fifty dollars. Mr. Kramer did not want any money for the ranch, instead he wanted fence posts. Charlie cut enough fence posts at three cents a piece to pay for his ranch in five days. Later he acquired part of the Bouse homestead by helping Mr. Bouse prove up on his land. That gave Charlie one hundred and twenty-one acres.

Charlie and Clara had seven children, Willie, Ruby, Jim, Violet, George, Dollie and Freda. Now in Charlie's golden years, he is surrounded by his family. Clara is in a rest home. Ruby is what her father calls his head swampier and she runs the household. Ruby bakes all their own bread and had just finished canning sixty-nine quarts of peaches on a wood cook stove. Violet and Jim live at home. Dollie and her son Joseph, live on the farm as does Willie, his wife Lois and three sons, Luther, Lester and Russel. The whole family works to care for the garden, chickens, goats and hogs that provide the food for this self sufficient family.

George has moved to Idaho where he is a mechanic for Cummins Diesel. Freda has moved to Louisiana, as far away from her family as Charlie once moved from his.

Charlie has done most anything to make a living for his family. He dug most of the local graves by hand since 1936. The whole family worked in the potato fields when they were quite young hand picking potatoes for Mike Roufs. Charlie would build fence, split rails, ranch work, you name it. He said he has done a lot on the barter system, and still does. He feels the problem with people today is that they are afraid of hard work. He believes neighbors should help neighbors.

Willie and his sons have taken over his fathers garbage collection business that he started in 1938. They still use their vintage 1947 Chevrolet truck to collect the garbage in Bieber, Nubieber and Lookout. It has proven to be a very successful venture. The old truck purrs like a kitten as Willie is probably one of the master mechanics of all time and keeps it tuned like a top. Willie has always been a genius with tools and can make most anything run, from antique clocks to antique cars and tractors.

Newspapers and radio are the Shepherds' communication. They have no use for television. They are so independent that the three clocks that sit side by side near Charlie's chair display the regular sun time. He does not believe in daylight savings time. He said it is a bunch of "hooey".

The weather man may learn a thing or two from this man of the mountains. He believes that if you kill a skunk in the fall and turn it over and can see its skin on the belly without disturbing the hair, it will be a mild winter. There may be lots of snow, but not very cold but if the skunk has lots of hair, we are in for a cold winter.

Watch the animals, if they get a heavy coat of hair it will be a cold winter. If the wood rats build their nests high up in the trees it will be heavy snow and if the squirrels pack lots of pinenuts it will be a long winter.

Some people believed that when Charlie first came to Big Valley that he was with the F.B.I., but he says it was because he always packed a gun. He says he still does, but he is not quite the crack shot he once was. While in the service he claims he could shoot twenty bulls eyes out of twenty shots at five hundred yards with a Springfield rifle. "I could shoot the eyebrows off a gnat at three hundred yards," he commented.

Charlie Shepherd.

Charlie only went to the third grade, so he is what you might call a self taught man, or the school of hard knocks. He only left the country he loves one time to go to his granddaughter's wedding in Boise, Idaho in 1985 and he could hardly wait to get home.

Big Valley honored this monarch of the Shepherd family by having him as grand marshall of the Big Valley Days parade in 1986.

Charlie attributes his long and healthy, pain free life to his daily ritual of breakfast. Every single morning he eats raw rolled oats with milk, three toes of garlic chopped fine and six spoonsful of honey.

Life is never boring on the Shepherd homestead.

Glorianne Weigand
September 1993

Wilcox Ranch Survives Mt. Lassen Eruption

A terrifying noise up the creek roused many out of their sleep. Others only noticed the dogs or horses being nervous and upset. People came screaming "Get out, get out!!!!!" Before you could ask what happened or why, a wall of mud and dirt like an ocean wave was coming down the creek. It had white foam on its top, roaring like a windstorm on the ridge. Lava rocks ran before it, trees fell in its path and were pushed ahead with the mud and water. What would have been a normal spring day in May 1915 soon was a hell on earth for the people of the beautiful Hat Creek area.

The mountain, Lassen Mountain, had erupted and was roaring and challenging homes, barns, livestock and humans that could not run fast enough to get out of its furious path.

Ranchers raced to turn their stock loose to fend for themselves. The eruption came during the night and people had retired for the evening. When the warning came they barely had time to get to higher ground. Some at the lower end of the creek had some warning. But the ones at the upper end were lucky to escape with their lives.

People ran, fearing for their lives, some were without shoes to protect their feet from the lava rocks. The flood was bearing down with all its fury upon them. Everyone scrambled to higher ground to watch the flood go by. The immense heat of the erupting volcano melted the snow pack and walls of water and mud brought trees tumbling down and boulders rolling. Anything that was in the path of the flood was consumed.

There had been grumbling from the volcano for quite some time. But this particular day the explosions were bigger and louder than they had been. People were beginning not to pay any attention to them and went on with their life as normal. The evening before dogs had whined and barked. The livestock were skittish, but people paid them no mind.

The families of Hat Creek had huddled together high on the hill through the night. Not knowing what their fate would be. Early in the morning before the sun rose they were thrilled to hear the sounds of roosters crowing and it gave them hope that there was something still alive.

As dawn approached the sun rose over a devastated land. Harvey Wilcox came limping into his neighbors, Wid Hall's. Harvey didn't have time to get his shoes on before the flood got to him and he started for high ground cutting across the lava bed, known as Devil's Half Acre. He cut his feet so badly that Wid Hall had to tie barley sacks around them.

Harvey had just began to settle on his homestead of Upper Hat Creek when Mt. Lassen erupted. Harvey had borrowed a team from his brother Harry and on the night of the flood he heard the horses run by his cabin. Afraid they might get into the barbed wire fence, he ran out to look. He had not taken time to pull on his trousers and shoes and when he got outside, he could hear the flood roaring down upon him. With no time to waste, he climbed through the fence and ran for high ground and when he looked back, his cabin was gone. Harvey hobbled on to the nearest hill thinking he might be the only one alive on Hat Creek. All they ever found of Harvey's belongings was a can of coffee, a bucket and a can of lard. Much later a suitcase was found.

Things weren't too bad at the Wilcox Ranch but the Hawkins family was hit hard. The Wilcox men started to help Hawkins clean out and there came another terrible explosion, so everyone left for Burney.

The land was covered with ashes and debris. Everyone on Hat Creek had dairy cows that had to be moved to pastures and cleaner areas. The next day they went back for their milk cows. They took Hawkins, Rube Wilcox and Opdykes cattle to the old Haynes place in Long Valley near Burney. The ninety cows had not been milked in two days so they stopped on the road and milked them. The three families had to move into the same house with several small children. The situation was hard, but could not be helped.

Before the second eruption occurred people were starting to move back into their homes. All bridges along Hat Creek had been torn out. They built foot bridges and rounded up their livestock. But then all was undone when the mountain blew its top again.

The Wilcox men, Mr. Reiger and Mr. Kirk had gone up to the Hawkins place to try to change the creek back to its old channel. The second flood came with less notice and more fury that the first. People raced to the ranger station for safety. They put their food in the attic and turned their stock loose, not knowing when they would find them or when the poor cows would get milked again. All the farmers had milk cows, so after they were rounded up again they were driven to Goose Valley where Harry Wilcox had rented a place. Charlie Opdyke milked sixty cows by hand over a week before anyone could get there to help him.

Life was hard for the Wilcox family as with any family in the early years. Sickness with no doctors close by, Indians were unfriendly and living at the foot of a live volcano only added to their problems.

In 1872 Charles W. Wilcox came to Hat Creek. He was born December 3, 1831 in New York. The gold rush had brought him to California, near Wheatland. But not to dig for gold but to run a freight line. While in Wheatland he met Emmeretta Parker and they were married December 13, 1861. Four children were born while they lived there, Naomi, Olive, Harvey and Charles. After they moved to Hat Creek, Reuben and Harry were born.

Charles took up a homestead along Hat Creek of 160 acres in 1872. Their living was made by milking cows and making butter to haul to Red Bluff and he had a few beef cattle. The trips to Red Bluff were not made but once or twice a year so the butter had to be preserved. A salt brine was made by adding salt to water until it would float an egg. Then the rolls of butter wrapped in cloth would be stored in barrels and covered with brine. They were kept in a cool spring house or covered with ice from the ice caves near Mt. Lassen.

The Wilcox children either married or went on to start a life of their own. Naomi married Lawrence Simpson and they had eight children. Olive married Jack Opdyke and they also had eight children. Harvey never married and took up a homestead near Old Station. Charles was sent to Red Bluff to school and took sick and died of pneumonia at fifteen years of age. Reuben inherited the original ranch and married Amy Kirk and had three daughters. Harry M. married Emma Spaulding and had six children.

When Harry was only six weeks old, Emmeretta took sick with milk fever. The closest doctor was at Fall River Mills. This was February and Pit River was at flood stage and the bridge had washed out. Long Tom, an Indian who had befriended the Wilcox family, ran the many miles to the Pit River, swam across the roaring water and ran on to Fall River Mills to get medicine from the doctor. Retracing his swim and his run he delivered the medicine to the Wilcox home, but too late to save Emmeretta's life. Baby Harry was shifted from family to family to be raised.

Another of the Indians that Mr. Wilcox was friends with was Shavehead, Long Tom's brother. He was the chief of the Hat Creek Indians and had been known to be very hostile and had the reputation of murdering more whites than any other Indian. Mr. Wilcox had paid Shavehead for his land instead of trying to take it from him as many settlers had. The land that he bought was the Hat Creek chief's headquarters and soon to be the Wilcox Ranch. Shavehead would visit the Wilcox Ranch and say to the women, good mahalia, little coffee, little sugar? They would give him supplies if he needed them.

Once an Indian was sent to scout a deal to kill Wilcox. He was treated with much kindness and given food to eat and a place to sleep. He went back to his tribe and said, "No kill that good white man."

Charles Wilcox died on the ranch in 1900 and his friend, Shavehead, died the same year at Deer Flat near Mt. Lassen.

Chester Wilcox & Goldie Wilcox (in chair).

Harry M. had met Emma Spaulding at a Christmas dance in Cassel. After a courtship of a year, they were married December 12, 1900 in Burney. Harry's father had died in March so they made their first home on the ranch. Before Emma married, she had finished school in Redding and had done housework for several different families.

Harry and Emma bought a homestead in Long Valley near Burney. Harry brought some special horses that his father had bred. They were called Kentucky Whip horses and some of them lived to be thirty years old.

Five Wilcox children were born in Long Valley. Bessie, Ialla, Chester, Emeretta and Harry D. The family then moved back to Hat Creek. Harry bought part of the home place and took a ten year lease on the rest.

In 1925, Harry and Emma bought the Charles Hawkins place at Hat Creek and moved there.

In 1904 the Bar WH brand was established and the Wilcox family started raising beef cattle along with their herd of milk cows.

Harry D. was born October 11, 1909. He was a lively child with bouncy red curls. Charlie Hawkins started calling him Goldie at an early age and the nickname followed him the rest of his life.

Goldie went to school at the Cassel School for his first few years and stayed with his teacher Irene Bidwell. He later went to the Wilcox School near the ranch and stayed at that school through the eighth grade.

Goldie's mother wanted him to go to Davis and take a dairy course, but he said he could not leave the ranch because his dogs would forget him and his horse needed him.

Goldie loved to read and loved his animals. He had many dogs that followed him through his daily chores. Harry M. died in 1930 at the age of fifty-two from pneumonia. Goldie promised his mother he would never leave the ranch and he would stay and take care of her.

Goldie had run many trap lines as a young man and did quite well with this enterprise.

December 14, 1931 Harry D. (Goldie) and Verna Greer were married in Medford, Oregon. Goldie had to sell his favorite cow to finance their wedding. The first thing the newlywed couple did after they were married was to climb Mt. Lassen. They would climb the mountain and slide down the snow.

Verna was born June 24, 1911 in Cayton Valley and lived in Burney until she was married. She was four years old at the time of the Mt. Lassen eruption and can remember the ashes falling in Burney and the Hawkins family came to Burney for safety. Her father, Fred Greer took his team and wagon to Hat Creek to help move the people and their belongings out. Her mother, Laura Sangster Greer, had met Fred Greer in Dana when she came there to teach. Her father bought a ranch in Cayton Valley then later bought one in Burney.

Goldie Wilcox.

Verna Wilcox.

Verna's mother traveled and taught school nine months out of the year and Verna traveled with her. Verna was taught all eight years by her mother. Her father stayed home and ran the ranch. Ellen, John and Fred were older and stayed home on the ranch with their father. Mr. Greer ran a freight line and when the bells of his freight wagons were heard it was an exciting time for the family that their father was home.

Verna graduated as valedictorian of her 1930 Fall River High School class. She went on to U.C. Davis to be a doctor, but fell in love with Goldie and they got married. Verna and Goldie moved into the large home on the Wilcox Ranch and started raising their family. Ellen Betty Wilcox Taylor, Verna Marie Wilcox Beck, Harry David Wilcox II and Cordelia Ruth Wilcox Saltzman.

Goldie's mother Emma, passed away in 1966 at the age of 88.

The depression hit and dust storms and drought hit the ranchers very hard. In 1931, the cattle had no feed so they fed them potatoes. They would cut the potatoes all up by hand to keep the cows from choking on them. Goldie was allowed 100% of the water from Hat Creek for irrigation but in that year he only received one third of the needed water. The Wilcox Ranch is around seven hundred acres, but not all of it was meadows and irrigated land. It had its share of lava flows and rocks.

The Hat Creek Stock Association minutes of March 29, 1939 show that the following grazing permittees assembled at the Hat Creek Ranger Station for the purpose of forming a stock association. Perry Opdyke, Harry Lonquist, E.B. Estes, H.D. Wilcox, C.M. Bidwell, R.E. Bidwell and Glenn Ratledge. R. Box was the ranger at the time and acted as secretary. All paid their fifty cents dues.

The minutes of 1940 stated that because 1939 was so dry the cattle were forced off of the range from July 1 to September 15. April 1 was the normal range opening date and October 15 the closing date. A lengthy discussion for vaccinating cows for abortion was held. Some did not want to monkey with the state veterinarian and said they would do their own vaccinating.

In 1941 Alan Brown and Dave Doyel joined the group. The members wanted to change the October 15 off date as they did not want to pay for the extra time as the cows were off the range anyhow.

The 1942 minutes ask for 25% of the range fees to be used on range improvements such as ponds and fences. The war was on and the government was broke and couldn't do any range improvements.

In 1943, A.L. Doty, Bill Austin, Scott Ratledge, C.E. Scott, Pat Kirkpatrick, Harry Lonquist and Dan Gellerman joined the association. They were happy for the fifty cent dues from each new member as their treasury was down to ninety-four cents. A special meeting was held in May regarding cattle rustling.

Goldie Wilcox, 1943.

In 1944, deer damage to the ranchers was devastating. A letter was sent to the California Cattleman Association asking them to propose a one dollar fee to be added to deer tags by the fish and game to build fence to help ranchers protect from the deer damage. Al Meeker, Ward Smith and Elmo Lonquist joined.

In 1945, Otto Giessner, Charles Heryford and Rudolph Giessner joined. Ken Fox was the new ranger at the Hat Creek Ranger Station.

In 1948, Floyd Bidwell joined. Floyd, along with Perry Opdyke and Al Meeker were to represent the association on the hide and brand law. At this time, Goldie Wilcox was the secretary. New members Jess Eldridge and Bill Spaulding joined and a discussion on joining the Fall River-Big Valley Cattlemen was held. This was a branch of the California Cattlemen's Association and the members felt it would be beneficial to belong to that organization.

In 1961, Ned Bognuda and George Corder joined the Stock Association. In 1958 a group of men decided it would be a good idea to organize a cattle sale at the Inter-Mountain fairgrounds for the local cattlemen. It was quite a ways to haul their cattle to an auction yard, so they would try a fall feeder sale. Some of the cattlemen that got the sale going were John McArthur, Goldie Wilcox, Albert Albaugh and Lem Ernest, among others. The sale proved a success and in the 1950's they tried a spring and fall sale, but there was not enough cattle in the spring to keep the sale going so after about four years they dropped it. The fall feeder sale by the cattlemen is still going strong and they market several thousand head of cattle on that one day with the help of all the cattlemen, the crew from the Shasta Livestock Market and the Cattlewomen serving a noon beef lunch.

Goldie Wilcox ran a pack string into the Thousand Lakes area for a while to pack fishermen in and out. Goldie loved to read and loved his family and animals. Ranching was in his blood and his life and he never wanted to do anything else. He raised good Hereford cattle and used some Durham bulls to cross breed his cows.

The main ranch was where Goldie raised his hay and wintered his cows and had a feedlot for his feeder calves. About five miles away is another part of the ranch, known as Lost Creek. This is meadows and lava flows and where the cattle are taken early in the spring. This is used as summer pasture for some while the rest of the cattle are driven on to the Forest Service for their permit there.

Harry D. "Goldie" Wilcox passed away in 1970 at 60 years of age. His wife Verna, was left to run the ranch. Their son, Harry stayed to help his mother for one year, but wanted to be a logger so moved to Idaho to pursue his occupation. He has one son in the Navy, Harry D. Wilcox III.

Norman and Betty Taylor moved to the ranch with their four young sons, Richard, Robert, Ralph, and Rodd. Later, a daughter, Ruth was born. Verna was happy to have her daughter and son-in-law move onto the ranch. She moved into the smaller house on the ranch and let them have the large home.

Norman still worked in his family business in McArthur, the Crum Meat Company, that was started by his grandfather Merton Crum. Norman, his brother Jack, and Uncles Hiram, Orville, Harold and Donald ran the slaughter plant and meat cutting business. The slaughter plant closed its doors and Norman went to work full time running the Wilcox Ranch. Betty is the Hat Creek post mistress, and Norman's partner in all the ranch business.

Verna's children, Betty, Marie, Harry and Cordelia, all have an interest in the Wilcox Ranch. Marie is the director of nurses at Mayers Hospital at Fall River and her children Cindy, Pam, David and Danny help out on the ranch whenever they can. Cordelia is the fourth grade teacher at Bieber and her children Andrea, Jessica and John enjoy the cattle drives and the haying.

One of Norman and Betty's sons, Ralph, lives on the ranch with his family and works there. His children are the sixth generation of Wilcox's to walk the land and fish in Hat Creek that flows clear and gently through the land.

Norman and Betty have made changes and the meadows have been leveled and planted to alfalfa and flood irrigated to produce three cuttings of hay. The hay is all put up by family members and is only used to feed the cattle there. No hay is sold. When the forest fire of 1987 came so close to the ranch, Norman let the water out in the fields of hay to keep the roaring flames from consuming the ranch. Some cattle were killed in the fire and some came home badly burned, but survived.

A new home was built a few years ago to replace the old home that survived the Mt. Lassen eruption when the Hawkins family lived in it. Plans are being made to some day make the Wilcox Ranch a guest ranch, for those people that would like to see what a real working cattle ranch is all about.

Because the ranch is in a lava area, the selenium is severely lacking in the soil and this makes the cattle very deficient, so they have to have supplemental selenium. Lepto has proven to be a serious problem in that area also. Most of the cattle are fall calvers which works best for the Wilcox Ranch. The Hereford bulls have recently been purchased at BB Cattle Company, in Washington. They buy shorthorn bulls from Frosty Acres in Adin and they buy angus bulls from their neighbor, Rancheria Angus for their first calf heifers. The cattle are marketed at the Fall River-Big Valley Cattlemen feeder sale in the fall and twenty head are entered in the Inter-Mountain Fair steer futurity and sent to a feed lot in Washington.

Verna Wilcox was a wealth of information for this article and at the age of 82 is still healthy. Even though she had a heart by-pass a few years ago, she recently completed a two mile walk for the Redding Medical Center, known as the Turkey Trot. She is duly proud of the ribbon she won, but attributes it to her three daughters and grandchildren that were at her side every step of the way urging her on.

The Wilcox Ranch has survived the Mt. Lassen eruption, Indians, droughts and fires. They are still going strong and it is people like Goldie and Verna Wilcox who made it so.

Glorianne Weigand
February 1994

There Was Never a Bronco Too Tough

In the small town of Adin, California in the county of Modoc is one of the nicest parks you'll ever picnic in. The retired park attendant Roy Swain took loving care of the park for fourteen years from 1970 to 1984. Roy's home is across the street from the park and neither an ugly dandelion or a piece of paper were allowed to enter his domain. This is what Roy is well known for in the last few years, but in his younger days a rougher, tougher, bronco buster was hard to find.

A more gentle or kind man you will never meet, and you would never suspect the rough and exciting life he has led. Roy has left his mark in the cowboy books of the wild west. He is also the last of the notorious Swain gang. The best bootleggers in the northwest territory.

Roy has led a long colorful life that started in Susanville, California, September 26, 1906 in his Uncle Henry's home at the end of Main Street that is now the Elks Hall.

Roy was born to Adelia Blair Swain and John Swain. Adelia had come across the plains in a covered wagon to the Madeline plains in Lassen County where her father ran a ranch. John's father had come from Texas to homestead in Madeline.

When it was near time for Roy to be born his mother went to Susanville to be near help when the baby arrived. Roy was the youngest of four boys and one girl. The girl died as an infant. One brother, Fred died in 1918 at the age of eighteen from the flu in the great epidemic. Roy, his brother Albert, nicknamed Ab, and William, nicknamed Dugan, were left to carry on the Swain name.

On a cold morning February 28, 1912 John Swain who was the company inspector on the phone line from Dry Valley to Grasshopper Valley headed out to do his job. He decided to take his five year old son Roy with him in the wagon. He had a saddle horse tied to the back of the wagon and the wagon was loaded with rolls of telephone wire. After he got to Dry Valley to meet the crew a dog ran out and heeled the saddle horse causing him to buck and snort around. This scared the team John was driving. He tried to control them, but they were soon charging at top speed. An uncontrolled runaway was in progress. John was concerned about the safety of his young son so he tossed him to the ground, then he tried to bring the frightened horses under control. The ground was rough and rocky and the horses were going at full bore. The wagon hit a bump that threw John ten feet in front of the wagon and the team and wagon ran over him, leaving him bleeding and unconscious on the ground. The team stampeded all the way back for several miles to the Swain Ranch tearing out several fences on the way.

The men in their attempt to catch the runaway came upon little Roy sitting in the dirt crying. He was only bruised and scraped. A little farther down the road they found John. They brought him back to consciousness. He asked the men to take him home, which they did.

They phoned for Dr. Smith at Bayley Creek seven miles away and he came on a long lope. The doctor found John Swain in a dangerous condition with fractured ribs, punctured lung and internal bleeding. Mr. Swain only lived a few hours leaving his wife Adelia with four sons between five and thirteen years old. Mrs. Swain moved to Reno for a few years. She later married Marvin Vann and moved back to the ranch for fifteen years.

Roy had his first job when he was sixteen as a buckaroo. He went to work for George and Elmer Williams for $60.00 a month and they furnished the horses. He loved to ride broncos but there was also always the job of haying in the summer and feeding cows in the winter.

In the early 1920's Roy went to work for the Corporation Ranch in Likely. There, Charlie Demmick was the boss and Roy stayed there for three years. There, he was paid $75.00 a month as he had more experience than the other cowboys. He also got his board and room. Roy describes Charlie Demmick as one of the greatest cowboys he ever worked for. Some of the bronc riders Roy rode with there, were George Brown, George Fuller and Westy Williams.

In 1927 Roy started working for the J.D. Flournoy Ranch in Likely. He stayed there for five years. Roy spent the winter in Jess Valley feeding cows and chopping ice for them to drink. The thermometer on the bunk house wall registered 46 degrees below zero. By sundown the mercury had gone clear out of sight and stayed that way for ten days. A foot and a half of snow was also on the ground. When Roy went to work for the Flournoys, Rob, Don, Harry and Warren were still in grammar school.

Roy tells about a lot of wild bronco rides and wild dances. While in Jess Valley he had a Model A Ford that all the cowboys would pile in on a Saturday night and off to the dances in Likely, Alturas, Madeline or wherever there might be some excitement.

Bob McGarva, Clyde Brooks and John French were some of Roy's buddies he rode and worked with. They lived in the bunk house with the cook house at the other end.

Roy Swain feeding cows at Jess Valley, 1927.

Roy started running wild horses with his rowdy cousins the Marr brothers on the Madeline plains. Harry, Brin, Bruce and Jim Marr and Roy were quite the rowdy bunch of horse wranglers. Roy loved to ride with the Marr boys. They would rope a horse's four feet throw him down, saddle him, get on and let the horse up for the wildest ride they could hope for.

Roy's wildest chase while running wild horses was when he spotted a wild mare with a beautiful black yearling at her side. Roy wanted that yearling real bad. At the time the Marrs and Roy were camped at Painter Flat and ran horses to the Buffalo Hills. They had been running the horses a while when Roy spotted the mare and colt. He ran her for miles and miles thinking he could lasso the colt when it got tired, but the mare outsmarted Roy and headed for a canyon and lost Roy in her dust. He never spotted the mare and colt again.

Lots of wild horses and lots of branded horses ran the wild Madeline plains. Marrs sold horses to the cavalry and at one time they shipped five hundred head of horses including colts to China. They loaded them on the train at Ravendale to go to San Francisco to be loaded on the boats.

Hippy Burmister, one of the cowboys Roy rode with turned out to be world champion bronco rider and now is in the Cowboy Hall of Fame. Hippy and Roy rode together to gather cattle at Mill Creek near Eagle Peak.

Out on the Madeline plains a severe drought was taking its toll. The economy had gone in a slump after the war which caused the deep depression. Cattle and sheep prices were down to nothing.

Although at this time there was one money-making business, bootlegging. Swain whiskey was known throughout the territory. Their still was located

Ben Colvis & Roy Swain, 1927,
at the Jess Valley bunk house.

in a difficult to reach concealed spot. "Jackass" as the bootlegged whiskey was called was produced more by the Swain brothers than any other outfit. Their clientele came from California, Nevada, Oregon, Utah, Washington and Arizona. Their whiskey was well known. Roy's brother Ab started a small still in the back of the Swain Ranch just for weekend parties when they would ride wild bronco's and drink.

There was money to be made in the moonshine business so the Swains went at it full bore. The still was located under a rimrock at the head of Pine Creek above Horse Lake. Allen Luddy and Hal Brown joined their operation. The huge still held 350 gallons of mash from which they could make 30 gallons of good whiskey in ten hours.

Roy Swain ran the supply line with a string of pack horses. He hauled the grain and sugar in to the still and hauled the whiskey out in ten gallon kegs. He hauled them to the ranch and buried them wherever he could until a buyer came along. The moonshine was put in gallon jugs for sale to the locals and sold for $10.00 a gallon. Wholesale prices for larger quantities was $8.00 per gallon.

The demand got so great that Roy's pack string could not keep up, so Ab and Hal decided to make a road. That move was a little too risky for Roy. If they were going to have a road the agents could follow, Roy wanted out. He quit the outfit and went back to buckarooing.

In 1928 not long after the road was built the federal agents drove right up to the still. Ab was fined $100.00 and given three years probation. As the feds chopped up the still and poured 350 gallons of whiskey on the ground they remarked "it was a shame to waste such good whiskey after all the rot gut they had found at other stills."

While Roy was working for the Flournoys, Kenneth Flournoy told him a rattlesnake would die if you spit chewing tobacco down its throat. Roy being a daredevil, he decided to give it a try. Roy caught the snake and held it down with some sagebrush sticks. Kenneth stuck some sticks in the snake's mouth so it couldn't bite them. About six inches from the snake's mouth he spit a chew of his star tobacco down its throat. The snake died. Roy still would not believe Kenneth because he thought the snake died because he had been roughed so much. A few days later they came upon another rattlesnake and Roy wanted to try it again. This time he was careful and soon as Kenneth spit down the snake's throat he died. Two times was enough to make a believer out of the young cowboy from Termo.

Roy was always good for a joke. He rode a big black horse that he roped a five point buck on and led him down the hill and put him in a cabin. He told a guy he could butcher the buck but he was so tough you could not even eat the gravy.

Ronald McGarva &
Roy Swain.

Roy Swain, 1930.

142

Don Tate and Montana Red a trick rider are among some of the famous cowboys Roy cowboyed with. Roy went southwest in Lassen County and worked on the Dixie Valley Ranch where he rode with Billy Denio and Ed Owens for the C.W. Clarke Company. Roy was a real hand with colts and knew the cow business real well so he was in demand wherever he wanted to cowboy.

In Dixie Valley he became good friends with the Bognuda girls, Clover and Lil. They rodeoed all over. Lil was an outstanding lady bronc rider in the rodeos in those days. While they were at Lakeview Roy's car, saddle, gear and all was stolen. His car was found in Washington but he never found any of his other belongings.

Roy only stayed at Dixie for a short time as J.D. Flournoy became sick and they asked him to come back to Likely to work. While in Jess Valley Roy met Edith Gordon who took his heart. Edith and Roy were married in Reno, Nevada January 16, 1935. Roy had seen enough cold winters alone. Edith had a daughter Rose Lea that Roy adopted when she was ten.

Edith was a cook for the Edgerton Bros. Lumber Company when they were at the Likely Mill. In 1937 Edgerton moved their mill to Adin and Edith went along to run a cook house and boarding house in the old Adin Hotel. At that time Roy was back at the Corporation Ranch and he stayed on for a few years.

In 1940 Roy and Edith moved to Sacramento and ran a ranch for Orin Hill. In 1944 they moved back to Adin and Roy prospected at the Hayden Hill gold mine for several years. Roy then decided to try the lumber mill business, but in 1960 a lift truck ran over him and he lost his leg.

Even with a wooden leg it did not slow that old bronco rider down much. He started back at ranch work, riding horses and haying, but gave up the broncos. Although he did buy a horse from Stan Weigand that liked to hump up a little each morning. Roy said he wanted something with a little life to it.

Roy worked for Tom Barrows for several years, then went to Ash Valley and worked for Lloyd Stone.

Roy then went to work for Modoc County taking care of the Adin Park for fourteen years. After Roy turned 78 years old he decided to retire.

Reading many good western stories which probably don't hold a candle to his own stories has been one of his favorite pastimes. His well-kept home and yard are a tribute to him.

Edith passed away October 23, 1988 after fifty-three years of marriage. Roy's family, many friends and wonderful memories of a life in the wild west keep him occupied.

Happy trails Roy from a friend who has enjoyed your wonderful stories.

Glorianne Weigand
July 15, 1993